A Handbook of Modern Arabic

Consisting of a Practical Grammar, with Numerous Examples, Dialogues, and Newspaper Extracts in a European Type

Francis William Newman

Alpha Editions

This edition published in 2020

ISBN : 9789354156076 (Hardback)
ISBN : 9789354153518 (Paperback)

Design and Setting By
Alpha Editions
www.alphaedis.com
email - alphaedis@gmail.com

As per information held with us this book is in Public Domain. This book is a reproduction of an important historical work. Alpha Editions uses the best technology to reproduce historical work in the same manner it was first published to preserve its original nature. Any marks or number seen are left intentionally to preserve its true form.

PREFACE.

ARABIC is talked differently in Algiers, in Malta, in Egypt, in Syria, in Bagdad, and among the Arabs of the desert. Nowhere[1] is the Arabic of the Koran and of poetry spoken. The difference of the old and new is similar in many respects to that between the Greek of Homer and the Greek dialects at the time of Xenophon. No modern can without pedantry and absurdity speak in the older dialect. When he composes poetry, he may write as Hariri, if he can; just as an Athenian or Alexandrian, if he chose to adopt dactylic hexameters, might use the dialect of Homer. When the Arab now writes prose, he closures the chasm which separates his dialect from the ancient, by omitting the vowel points, which used to distinguish the *cases* of the noun and the *moods* of the verb. While learned men struggle to forbid the phrase Modern Arabic, and will have it that the language has not changed (as if change were not a necessity of nature and a condition

[1] See P.S.

of growth), they yet distinctly confess that these final vowels are not and may not be sounded. But their omission so mutilates the old grammar, as in itself to constitute a new dialect. Moreover the words in use have largely changed, especially those in most frequent recurrence. A huge mass of meanings have become obsolete. The dictionaries mischievously heap together, without distinction, the senses which belong to different ages or places, and call that "Arabic." Even concerning the Thousand and One Nights, which is more recent than the age esteemed classical, the learned Mr. Lane confesses that it is often impossible, "out of twenty or more significations which are borne by one Arabic word," to be sure which was intended by the author. He declares that the style of that book is neither classical, nor is it that of familiar conversation, but is almost as different from the one as from the other. I hope that I need no further defence for insisting that to learn the Modern Arabic is not to learn the Ancient, and to learn the Ancient is not to learn the Modern.

Although the local dialects differ considerably, the difference is superficial, as in other cases of provincialism. When Arabs write a very unpretending letter, they lay aside a part of their local peculiarity. Mercantile letters from Syria to Bagdad, or Bussora, or Tunis, are a rough representation of "Modern" Arabic, as distinct on the one hand from the purely local dialects, on the other from the classical language.

PREFACE. vii

Catafago's English-Arabic Dictionary evidently aims at this mark. A fuller and far richer exhibition of the same is in the Arab newspapers; which, whether published in Algiers or at Beirout, are in a dialect and style closely alike. To this may be added numerous publications of recent years, which exhibit the Arabs struggling to put off provincialism, and assume a common medium of thought. Such is what I understand by Modern Arabic, only its want of vowel-points leaves many minor problems unsolved. If any one has urgent need to understand Lancashire talk, he must go into Lancashire to learn it: so he must go to Algiers, or to Aleppo, to learn the local dialect. But if he wish to learn English, he will do best to learn first, neither the jargon of our peasants, nor the poetry of Spencer or Chaucer. Such easy prose or familiar language as educated Englishmen use, must be his beginning. He will afterwards go with advantage into any special field of English. The same applies to Arabic.

A peculiarity of the present Hand-book is its systematic preference of a European type, and its effort to put that type on a basis which should remove all objection to its permanent use. This has been a favourite object with the writer for more than the third part of a century, after his early experience of the great and needless difficulties which the current imperfect mode of writing Arabic involves. He did not then know that Volney had long since promulgated the same doctrine: but the moment that a European understands the nature of the case, it needs not even experience to show the hardship now gratuitously inflicted on the learner. What would be thought of an English teacher's common sense, if, when a Frenchman desired to learn English, he should insist on teaching it him by a form of writing which omitted short vowels? Nay, if a Frenchman, ignorant of English, desired to read English short-hand, we should regard it as an insanity in him to refuse to learn our language and our long-hand *first*. If any one deny this, further argument is useless. The sole real question is that of fact: *does* the current literature omit vowels? It does, except for poetry; and the vowels of poetry do not show the actual pronunciation of prose and of cultivated speech. At present a learner is thrown on the dictionary, to fix many of the vowels: and since in learning languages we must forget much, and we remember only by frequent repetition, he may have to look out in his dictionary ten times, to know how to pronounce one word, even if the context show him its meaning. Then, alas! the best modern dictionary (. . . . . . author) is seldom pointed: in consequence of which, as I am now aware, I used often to put wrong vowels to the words which I learned from that dictionary. When the gram-

Only French-Arabic: one cannot look out an Arabic word in it; nor indeed in Catafago, with his alphabetic arrangement.

matical analysis of a word is already known, grammatical rules will often settle the short vowels; but how to analyze the word, is perhaps the very problem to be solved; or whether the word is to be active or passive, is doubted. Moreover, so few of the people are educated, that their enunciation is very obscure. To learn the true vowels by the ear, is to the foreigner all but impossible. When the books and even the dictionaries alike evade to inform him, whence is he to learn? Grant that every one will wish *ultimately* to read the native short-hand; still, the speediest way to attain the power, is, by first learning the language in long-hand, exactly as if we were dealing with English.

Some years back I printed a hand-bill on this subject, exhibiting a system of European transliteration, and closing with the following passage:—

"IV. ADVANTAGES OF A EUROPEAN TYPE.—1. It will split the difficulties to Europeans learning Arabic, and to Arabs learning a European tongue. We shall be able to grapple, first with the language, and *afterwards* with the Arab type, and the Arab conversely. 2. What in contemplating new literature is of high importance,—it will lessen the expense of printing. 3. It will give to the Arabs capital letters, Roman letters and Italics; for many reasons valuable, especially in facilitating reference by a mere glance of the eye, and in preventing proper names from being mistaken for unknown common words. 4. By a more perfect punctuation, and by quotation marks, our type has advantage over even the most carefully pointed Arab text, in ease and quickness of reading. Much greater is its advantage in ease and certainty over an unpointed text. 5. It will aid foreigners and natives to enlarge their vocabulary. At present, with an unpointed text, even the native is apt to make ridiculous or disgusting blunders, if he dare to put vowels at random to a word previously unknown. 6. It will enable Arabs to write foreign names unchanged, or nearly unchanged; as Europeans do. Now, their attempts at foreign names are ludicrous, and involve enormous error. 7. Small Arab types strain the eyes of readers painfully; an important topic to Bagdad, Syria, and Egypt, where weak eyes and blindness are so terrible a scourge. 8. Few of even professed scholars ever gain the same intimate familiarity with an alphabet totally foreign, as with their own. If the Arabs need European instructors,— if they need Europeans to co-operate in producing for them a new literature, (*without which they can have no national resurrection,*)—they must be willing to accept our alphabet. By it they will multiply a hundredfold their aid from Europe, and will facilitate their own access to European literature. 9. By duly writing the double system of vowels, the imagination of Arab readers will be set more upon them, to the certain softening of Arab elocution, and a great lessening of its fatigue. At present, from the habit of writing consonants only, the intense effort to distinguish them leads to a spasmodic and hideous harshness, quite needless when the distinctive vowel sounds are duly heard. 10. So also the foreigner, who often proves permanently unable to execute some of the consonants correctly, will yet,—by cultivating the vowel sounds carefully, in which he is more apt,—attain a pronunciation always intelligible, never ridiculous, and at a short distance will seem to speak correctly. For vowels are heard further and clearer than consonants. 11. Whatever develops intellect, excites zeal for research into antiquity. A really new Literature, in European type, under European influence, will not make the students of the old literature fewer; but will enable them to pursue it more fruitfully, with minds more powerful to select and to fuse."

I distributed this hand-bill in many quarters, and received several letters. One learned gentleman briefly replied, that he "could not see any use in my proposed change,"—entirely ignoring the eleven uses which I had enumerated. Similar rebuffs came from other quarters. I suppose, therefore, I must count on nothing but opposition from the learned, who seem to me disposed much to underrate the difficulties which they have surmounted, or indisposed to smooth the way of learners. When the field of learning is infinite, it is with me a crime to increase difficulty. I do not write for the learned, but to aid the unlearned: hence I appeal to the latter alone;—to those who have good sense, but no acquaintance with this particular language.

I have been a learner of languages for more than fifty years past, and have learned much of a few languages, a little of many. I know what makes them easy, and what hard : and I positively attest that this Arabic type is an enormous and gratuitous increase of difficulty; pre-eminently as to words in which the vocalization is really uncertain,—in which case one is ever learning and unlearning, and wrongly (perhaps) blaming one's memory. It is astonishing that either protest or reasoning should be needed on a matter so plain. Suppose us not to be learners, but already learned. We take up a book,—say, a newspaper, and try to read it. To put the right vowels is impossible, until the eye has glanced forward in the sentence; for it may contain half a dozen words with doubtful vowels, which can only be adjusted by studying the whole. If the three words A, B, C be doubtful, each depends on the other two, as well as on the words which have no doubt. For instance,[1] *In ceteb*, means, If he shall have written; *Enna ceteb*, That he has written; *In cotib*, If it shall have been written; *Enna cotib*, That it was written; *Enna cotob*, That books—; and *Inna cotob*, Verily books—or—As for books—: and which of these is correct, depends on what is coming. The text writes all six perfectly alike. Thus every time one refers to a sentence, *it has to be studied anew.* The paper generally blots, if one try to insert vowel points in ink: hence I find it takes less time to write out in full, with my own pen, a work which I want to study, than refer to the unpointed Arabic text. Why natives make light of this, it is not my part to explain: but, whatever facility they have, it is none the easier to foreigners. If, then, we (or illiterate natives) desire to become expert in the short-hand, it is wise *first* to learn the language thoroughly in *long*-hand. At present it is difficult or impossible to get prose works that have the vowel points marked. The deficiency of stops, the absence of parentheses, and the mingling of words, aggravate other difficulties.

[1] It may also be read, *Enn, ceteb*, He groaned, he wrote.

PREFACE.   xiii

The task which I have taken on myself cannot be done perfectly by me. If a learned Arab could have enthusiasm for it, and had (as perhaps some may have) as keen an ear for the English, French, and Italian sounds as I have; and had been educated in European grammar as I have; and knew as well as I, where Europeans are apt to go wrong, and what they need;—he would execute this task better than I. No foreigner can know, in delicate cases, what vocalization is, on the whole, best—neither pedantic nor vulgar. I can but *collate* the pronunciations sanctioned by Faris, by C. de Perceval, by Cherbonneau, by De Braine, by Léon and Hélot, side by side with my own reminiscences and my own MSS. written in Syria and Bagdad, making allowance for a French ear, and the peculiar deficiency of certain simple short vowels in French. After all, the delicate cases are few and exceptional. I am obliged to give directions for pronunciation, and my directions have no pretence to be perfect. But if they could be perfect, they would still be insufficient. No Englishman can learn from a book to pronounce French correctly, and the same is true of Arabic, whether a native write it, or a foreigner.

The educated natives themselves vary among themselves, especially concerning the *fine* and *coarse* vowels; a distinction which exists, but is not acknowledged in writing, even when vowel points are added. Between *a* and *e* there is often much uncertainty; as, whether

xiv PREFACE.

to say Jadied,[1] f. Jadieda (new), or Jedied, f. Jediede: but it is no more important than the question whether *command, basket*, should be pronounced with the broad Italian *a* of Middlesex, or with narrow *a*, as in midland and northern counties. In some of these details I perhaps have not attained consistency of spelling. Nevertheless, not only is our vowel system immeasurably superior to theirs, but as regards types for consonants, our resources are really great. Greek gives us three letters, Θ Δ Γ, identical with ث ذ غ. Hebrew (a square type, easily harmonized with the Roman,) gives four letters, עחצט, identical with ط ص ح ع. English, in C Q X, has three superfluous letters; we may add long Z of old English. It only remains to use such resources judiciously.

In India European types are extensively used to write the native languages. Our missionaries employ them in Africa, in the Pacific, and everywhere else, with more or less skill. The objections urged by some of the learned are astonishingly superficial, such as, that it is "against the genius of a language to bring in a foreign alphabet." They might seem to think that the Arabic alphabet had grown out of the soil with the language. Notoriously, it was adapted from the Cufic, by the very clumsy method of points, such as we often employ upon Roman letters. The single Phœnician alphabet has been modified into Greek,

[1] In Aleppo I always heard Jedied, in Bagdad (I think) Jadied.

Coptic, Gheez, Amharic, Etruscan, and Roman; also into Estrangelo-Syrian, Cufic, Syriac, Samaritan, Hebrew, and Arabic. Very few languages indeed have had an alphabet made for their express use; and if there were more such, they would only vex us the more.

Volney suggested the right thing, but his characters did not at all harmonize with Roman type. The letters ought to adapt themselves also to Italics, and be easy for joining hand, if possible. To *dots* there are grave objections. A single dot cannot be large enough to strike the eye, without being ugly: the printer therefore is sure in the long run to make it hurtfully small. Also in MS. it easily looks like a blot, and mistakes arise as to which letter it is meant to affect; hence it impedes quick writing. A zero is better than a dot; yet this blots in writing, and is not so good as a continuous train of the pen. Besides, as I now know, unless a printer cut new types, the zero pushes the letters apart. Accents, and the apostrophe, are wanted for their own purposes, and in maps all such things are mischievous. If new types *must* be cut, it is well to make the forms as perfect as may be.

The objects to be gained by a system of European transliteration are so great, that the eleven arguments quoted above rather allude to than develop them. Something more must be here added. A sound knowledge of geography lies at the basis of modern culture, and for it MAPS are necessary. Without this knowledge the Orientals must remain as children, with weak, empty, and delusive ideas concerning other nations; incapable of receiving instruction by books or newspapers. But who will engrave maps for Turks, Arabs, and Persians in the type of their native MSS? what publisher in Paternoster Row or New York will undertake the speculation? And if such maps existed, what native seeking information would be able to read them, traversed by dots innumerable in irregular directions? An Arab may afford to turn into embroidery sacred texts with which he is familiar: but if one interlace in a map foreign names unknown to him, they must be unintelligible in such a character. Only maps with a very few names, such as are in our children's schools, could be legible. The Arab vowel points, utterly insufficient as they are to express foreign names, would entangle the problem worse than ever; for, the objections to using them and to dispensing with them are alike powerful. But we may further ask, Is INDIA never to receive modern cultivation? or is any one insane enough to suggest that the English Government will go to the expense of maps in the Devanagari and Tamil character?—a character far less embarrassing than that of Arabia. It will be replied,—" *Of course* all Indians who desire western cultivation must learn to read the names on European maps." By the same reason we are claiming nothing great, in expecting

Arabs to make themselves masters of two kinds of type, and learning to transliterate. Most evident is it, that the world cannot afford to indulge in separate atlases for Arabia, for Bengal, for the South of India, for Burma, for China. For all these peoples a prerequisite of cultivation is, to learn the *characters* and use the maps of Europe. Not indeed our *languages*; that would be a condition too hard to fulfil, a condition which no despot could enforce. But if a beneficent Sultan were to establish schools for Arabs, and were to teach Arabic in them through a European type solely, this could not be felt as a hardship, in a country where so very small a fraction of the natives can put right vowels to the simplest native text.

And this seduces me into a political remark. England at vast expense sustains an embassy at Constantinople, and a fleet in the Mediterranean, for the sake (it is said) of *English interests* in the East. When we inquire what interests are intended, nothing else is discoverable but that we desire to maintain in Turkey "good will to our commerce, our religion, and our communications with India." Men not the least acute in the English Parliament have avowed their belief that our diplomacy and our fleets have no tendency to promote this "good will," but rather the contrary. Without venturing on so large a question, one may be permitted to assert, that if half the expense of our Mediterranean fleet were retrenched, and the money spent under the direction of our CONSULS in free schools for the native population of Turkey,— to instruct them in Geography and the elementary knowledge to which it is the key, by the intervention of the European character and European maps;—it would do more in fifteen years to promote the intelligence and prosperity of Turkey, and with it all the solid and legitimate interests of England, than ambassadors and fleets can do in five hundred years.

P.S.—Since the above was in the printer's hands, I have seen the remarkable statements of Mr. Palgrave, that in the N. E. of Arabia, which he has opened to our knowledge, the people preserve in daily talk the final vowels of classical Arabic. Since no discussion of such a topic can here find place, it must suffice to remark, that if the people of that region talk the language current 1300 years ago in Mecca, it is now a strictly local peculiarity. In no case can the population, spread over the vast surface hitherto known, adopt the ancient dialect, as to its final vowels, or as to words and their current senses.

CONTENTS.

PART I.—ON PRONUNCIATION AND WRITING.

SECT.		PAGE
1.	Vowel Sounds	1
2.	Consonant Sounds	5
3.	Relations of Vowels to Consonants	11
4.	Process of Transliteration	16

PART II.—ON GRAMMAR.

1.	Nouns and Adjectives	19
2.	Composite State of Nouns	33
3.	Demonstratives and Emphatic Pronouns	39
4.	Interrogatives	46
5.	Prepositions	48
6.	Suffix Pronouns	54
7.	Auxiliary Nouns or Quasi Pronouns	60
8.	Numerals	64
9.	Plurals of Nouns and Adjectives	68
10.	Comparatives	73
11.	Relative Pronouns	75
12.	Elements of the Verb	80
13.	Types of the Noun	86
14.	Auxiliary Verbs	89
15.	Classes of the Verb	93

SECT.		PAGE
16.	Degenerate Verbs	99
17.	Adverbs and Conjunctions	104
18.	Ancient Cases of the Noun	109

PART III.—PRAXIS.

1.	Tables of Plurals	114
2.	Exercises on "*of*"	118
3.	Small Talk without Verbs	120
4.	At the Close of a Journey	122
5.	At the Caravanserai	124
6.	On Dessert	127
7.	Talk with a Cook on Catering	130
8.	With Muleteers on a Journey	133
9.	Coptic Feast	142
10.	Two Tradesmen	148
11.	Clothier and his Customer	152
12.	With a Tailor	155
13.	A Stationer with a Paper Merchant	158
14.	Specimen of Prose with few Verbs	161
15.	Newspaper Extracts	162

HANDBOOK OF MODERN ARABIC.

PART I.— PRONUNCIATION AND WRITING.

§ 1. VOWEL SOUNDS.

1. Pronounce *a* ordinarily as in *mutăble, coachmăn*, or nearly as *u* in *mud*. Thus, Bann, coffee-bean; Madd, he stretched; Rabb, lord; are sounded as English *bun, mud, rub*.

Yet with strong h (ḥ) and Ain (ᴛ) the *a* is sharpened into French *a* of *salon*; which happens in some other words not easy to enumerate, as Ana, I; Ẋahr, back (sound it, An-a). Perhaps *h* in Ẋahr, affects the *a*.

2. Short *e* is for the most part sounded nearly as in *měn, běll*, only not quite so clear. (Whether indistinctness is here any virtue, may be judged differently in different provinces.) Thus, Jĕb-al, a mountain; Bĕl-ad, a district; Mediena, a city; Ceb-ier, great. [The Englishman must not pronounce Jū-bal, Bēlad, nor M*i*diena, C*i*bier.] Thus also, El, the; Tell, hill; Ente, thou; Emte, when? Bel, but.

Nevertheless, *e*, like *a*, in many words takes a second sound, viz., that of English *a* in *man*, which is a sound not normal

1

in French and Italian. This sharpened sound of *e* may be heard especially, (1) in connection with *c* or *h;* as in Ecbar, greater; Ecθer, more; Lec, to thee: where Lec is to be sounded as English *lack,* and Bec (in thee) like English *back*. (2) In certain contrasts, such as Néfes, breath, Nefs, self; Béred, hail, Bard, cold; the second *e* of the dissyllable is sharpened so that an Englishman might write Nef-as, Ber-ad. Indeed in Ṭásel, honey, I always heard the *e* as our sharp *a*.

3. If certainty could be attained, it might be well to write *à è* for the sharper sounds of short *a* and *e;* thus we should have Àna, I; Ẑàhr, back; Entè, thou; Beràd or Berèd, hail; Bèc, in (or with) thee. I awhile attempted this, but found too many doubtful cases, and too much uncertainty whether I was pursuing laws of the language or provincial accent. On the whole I think that ՙ, *h*, and *c* tend to modify *e* into sharp English *a*, as ṭ tends to sharpen *a:* thus ՙEm, or; ՙEmma, but; ՙEmr, affair. There are not less than four different sounds of these two short vowels, which the Arabs either omit, or express by the single mark which they call Fatḥa.

4. Long *a* (â) is at least as broad as in *father, mask,* of the South of England. Indeed with Q the â is apt to take the deep sound of our *au aw* in *haul, bawl*. So too in the word Allâh, God, which an Englishman would be apt to write Ul-lauh.

5. Long *e* (ê) is as the vowel in *dare, bear, hair, their, there*. It is probably old Greek η, nearly French *é*, or *ê*. Many English families or even counties so mince the *a* in *grasp, basket, castle, command,* as to yield the sound of this ê; but in the South of England it is only heard before *r*.

6. Short *i* is as with us in *little pin*. This sound being unknown to the French (who are prone to say *leetle peen*), one is apt to be misled by French notation which aims to transcribe Arabic. In Min, from; Li, to; Tilf, waste; Mel-ic, king; Sinn, a tooth; Mafrib, sunset; Menzil, lodging; the short *i* is as clear as in English. [In many words the vulgar are quite indistinct, merging it in *o, u,* or *e*. Thus I always heard Belâ, without; which Faris writes Bilâ for the English learner. The word is a modern formation; but analogy requires Bilâ, so I follow Faris. And in some other words, in spite of provincialism, I cling to the classical *kisra*, where we have classical guidance.] Observe,—*never* to pronounce final short *e* as *i*.

7. Long *i* is as in English *machine*. It may be written *í* to save space; but to economize the circumflex, I write *ie* for it, as in our *field*. Thus Tien, figs; Mediena, city; Fetiele, wick [not F*i*tiel*i*, rather Fet-ielè].

8. Short *o* is ordinarily as our *oo* in *good*. Yet when accented in a closed syllable it is rather the French *o*, as Octób, write thou; Kobz, bread.

9. Our long *o* in *stone*, according to Catafago, is not Arabic at all. Yet the Christians and Jews in Aleppo pretty clearly say *Yoam*, a day (with the vowel sound of English *boat*); so *Loan*, a colour, etc. In strictness this is a Diphthong. English *oa* is only an approximation to it, yet it is an approximation which will never be misunderstood. In fact, there are here two sounds, which I write *eu, au*. Of these *eu* approaches to *oa, o* in *boat, bone,* and *au* to *ou* in *our, sound*. The Arabic utterance is here less pure and single than the English; two vowels are heard in imperfect combination

Thus Yeum, day (nearly Yoam), Dau, buttermilk (nearly Dow). In fact Dawâ, medicine, is sounded exactly as English Dow-a [compare *dower*], and might in Arabic be written Daua without impropriety.

10. Short *u* is intended for French *u* in *bureau*. In Syria both *o* and *i* often degenerate into *u;* especially when *o* is repeated. Thus they say Cutob for Cotob, books; Jubon for Jobon, cheese; Fulfol for Folfol, pepper; Muxmox for Moxmox, apricots.

11. Dotted *ö* represents the German sound, nearly French *eu* in *heureux, jeune*. In Syria *u* is often corruptly sounded *ö*, as FöΛΛa, for FuΛΛa, silver; Ḧöʃân, for Ḧuʃân, horse.

12. By *ui* I represent the long French *u* in *lune*, perhaps old Greek υι.

13. The diphthong *ou* is to be sounded as in French, or in English *you*. This might be written *û* to save space; but the fewer circumflexes the better.

14. The diphthong *öu* is a very obscure sound, but perhaps is that of French *oeu* in *soeur*, sister. Compare old Ionic ωυ.

15. The diphthong *ai* is very near to English *i* in *fire, tile;* as Kair, good; Kail, horses; Γair, other. No one can be misunderstood, or can seem absurd, who exactly utters here the English vowel. Yet the Mohammedan Arabs give somewhere more of the double sound.

16. The same remark applies to the diphthong *ei*. Nevertheless it is all but identical with English *ei, ey*, in *veil, grey*, which is the same sound as in *maid, pale*. Thus Leil, night, would be written Lale, or Lail, or Leyl by an Englishman. The combinations *ie, ui; ei, ai; ou, öu; eu, au;* might with equal grammatical propriety be written *iy, uy; ey,*

ay; ow, ow; ew, aw. But such notation would probably be less acceptable to Western readers.

§ 2. CONSONANT SOUNDS.

17. There are twenty-eight consonants. I call seven masculine or coarse; seven feminine or fine; fourteen neuter or medial. The neuters are—six liquids, l, m, n, r, w, y; three aspirates, θ, k, ſ; also the five letters f, b, d, j, x.

18. The liquids are sounded exactly as in English, if you carefully retain everywhere for *r* its full vibration (as in the Irish mouth), even before a consonant, or at the end of a word: as in Barr, terra firma; Bard, cold, *subst.* [for which an Englishman is prone to write Burrad, as though it were a dissyllable].

19. Of the aspirates, Θ is as in Greek, or English *th* in *thin, breath.* K, Γ are commonly written Kh, Gh; the former being German *ch* in *auch*, or rougher still, as in Switzerland. Γ is to K exactly as B to P, D to T. Arabic Ghain (Γ) is fundamentally the modern Greek Γ or Dutch *gh*, only exaggerated. It is our Northumberland "burr," the consonant heard in gargling. Many Frenchmen and Germans lisp R into Γ; hence Hanoteau (in Zouave) treats the Ghain as a modified R: but this obscures its relation to the aspirated K. In fact, R, K, Γ, are all alike vibratory, and Γ has no more of R than this common property. The Arabs say Tefarfor (TEΓAΡΓOR) for gargling the throat; a word suggested by the sound.

In MS. I am accustomed to write G g for Arabic غ and K k for خ; which involves no inconvenience while we deal with Arabic alone. But for certain languages into which Arabic enters,—as Zouave, Persian, Turkish,—this is objectionable; since G is there wanted for its English sound; and it seems a pity to waste Greek Γ, when we have it to our hand. Even in Arabic, English G is often useful for writing proper names; as in Giâna (*Guiana*), Gienia (*Guinea*), Ingliez (*English*), Ingilterra (*England*). Indeed in a few Arab nouns the English hard *g* is heard: thus Nargiel for Narjiel, cocoanut; Dongola, a heron. It is regarded as a peculiarity of the Egyptian dialect always to harden the Jiem (ج) into Giem, which is an approach to Hebrew. But no further notice will be here taken of this.

20. F, b, d, j, are sounded as in English: only perhaps the *d* is slightly dental, as with French and Italians. For *j* the French write *dj*, the Germans *dsch*, which are too clumsy for transliteration, and grammatically objectionable, especially when the letter has to be doubled. Finally, *x* here represents English *sh*, as in Portuguese, not without historical excuse; for *x* of Latin stood for Greek ξ, and the representative of this in Phenician and Egyptian seems to have degenerated into the *sk* and *sh*. But convenience is here the chief argument. We cannot afford to waste the *x*.

21. P and V are found only in foreign words, as Vâpour, a steamboat, which will probably prove an inevitable noun. Marceb-a-nâr, (fireship) suggests a different thing. In such names as Petersburgh, Paris, Vienna, Valparaiso, we need P and V. [Also in Persian, Turkish, Zouave, the sounds of English *tch* and French *j* are found, as well as the hard English *g*. These three are all marked in Turkish type by a *triple dot* (٭) which in MS. is habitually imitated by the

circumflex (᷶). A triple dot has none of the disadvantages in printing which a single dot involves. It is not mistaken for a blot on the MS.; and it is legible without being so large as to appear an ugly spot in the types. Hence I think that c, j, g surmounted by a triple dot will not ill represent ج, ژ, ګ, if occasion require, in Indian or African languages. Nevertheless, if Γ ſ be adopted for غ, our simple G g suffices for Persian Gaf.]

22. The seven feminine or fine consonants are s, z, t, ∆, c, h, ʾ. S never has the sound of z, but is everywhere sharp. T is slightly dental, and in Algiers tends to degenerate into *ts*, as with the Kabails or Algerine Berbers. ∆ ∆ is as in modern Greek, or our flat *th* in *the, this*. C is nearly our *k*, but forwarder in the mouth, and more mincing; as is the the case with *s, z, t* also. The Turks interpose short *i* after *c*, saying nearly (in English orthography) kican or kyean for cên. But the Bedouins sound *c* as our *ch* in *chill, chant, latch*; and the learner who has no opportunity of hearing the true sound of Q will do best to give to C its Bedouin pronunciation; otherwise he will almost inevitably confound it with Q. Even at Bagdad the Bedouin sound prevails, at least before *e* and *i*, and it is in perfect analogy with the soft sound of *j*, which is almost universal beyond Egypt. H is perhaps identical with English *h*. Finally ʾ (which is called Hamze) is a mere *hiatus*. We are made aware of it even in English, when we distinguish "an ʾice pudding" from "a nice pudding;" but an Arab would wish to write Antiʾochus, Itâliʾa, where it seems to us absurd to reckon the hiatus as a consonant. In such a word as Yesʾel (he asks), the consonantal power of the hiatus is less obscure.

23. Between *á* or *é* and *a* the Hamze in modern pronunciation generally becomes *y;* thus Mirsêʔa (anchor) is Mirsêya. Even Maʔ (water) is pronounced Mây; and so we may write it, the radical letters being *mwy*. The Mohammedans make Hamze audible in Xaiʔ (thing). Sometimes the Hamze between vowels changes to *w* (and is so written by the Arabs), especially when the preceding vowel is *o* or *ou;* as Mowellif (a composer) for Moʕellif.

24. The seven masculine or coarse consonants correspond with the feminine, each to each. They are Ꙅ, ʒ, Ⲧ, Ⲍ, q, Ḥ, Ṱ; Ꙅ, ʒ, Ⲧ, Ⲍ, Q, Ḥ, Ṱ. The two first are a pouting *s* and *z*. The lips are protruded, and (natives say) the tongue must be put between the teeth, with much danger of biting it. The form of Ꙅ is borrowed from Hebrew צ. The coarse *t* (Ⲧ) is familiar to us in Irish brogue, when *water* is pronounced. The upper gums (or even the palate) must be touched by a *broad* mass of the tongue, and the lips opened; while in the fine *t* the *root of the tooth* is touched by the mere *point* of the tongue, and the lips drawn closer. The Ⲍ is nearly *dth* of Englishmen, yet it is not a double sound, but a coarse ᐃ formed by a thick tongue on the gum; while in fine ᐃ the tongue delicately touches the edge of the fore tooth. Q is far deeper in the throat than our *k* (as *c* is forwarder in the mouth than *k*), and is very soft,—*wholly free from vibration.* The foreigner finds his throat soon to become sore at the root of the tongue from a frequent utterance of Q. It is thought to be heard from the rooks when they say *caw;* hence Qâq (pronounced Qawq) is Arabic for the crow, generically. Strong *h* (Ḥ) is often heard from Irishmen. It is wheezing and guttural, with something of a *w* in it at the beginning of a

word, as in our rare name Whewell. The force of air in the throat is considerable, and is strangely prolonged when it ends a word, as Melieh (good), Râh (he went). The letter Ain (ᶜ) is not merely a hiatus, like Hamze, but a muscular upward jerk of the chest and stomach, accompanied with an elevation of musical note to the vowel. It may be called a *spasmodic emphasis*, such as a stuttering man executes, when at last his vowel struggles out; as ᶜarab (Arabs), Maᶜz (goats), Robᶜ (quarter). A foreigner at first believes it is a vowel: and it is as much a semivowel as *s*, *st*, *h*, which we seem able to sound by themselves. Grammatically it is treated as a pure consonant.

25. In a few words either there is confusion between ʒ and ᶞ, or ʒ has changed its sound. Ƶàhr (the back), Ƶöhr (noon), Ƶölme (darkness), Naᶞuif (clean), ᵀaᶞm (bone); and in Syria ħafaᶞ (he preserved);—are pronounced with ᶞ, though written (in Arab character) with ʒ (ظ). But ʒâlim (tyrannical), ʒalm (tyranny), are sounded with ʒ, as though it were a different root from Ƶölme (darkness). [In classical dictionaries Naᶞuif is *dirty*, and Naʒuif, *clean !*]

26. The terminations -icq, -ich, -ieᶜ, are uttered as if a short *a* were interposed before the final consonant. [This is Patħa *furtive* of Hebrew.] It is peculiarly important in expressing -ieq, as ᵀaticq (ᵀatié-aq), *old;* since it at once discriminates Q from C. Possibly -ich, -ouh equally have the furtive *a*. The learner must most carefully learn to distinguish the terminations -ieᶜ, -ich, -ich, as in Xanieᶜ, shameful; Melieh, good; Cerieh, unpleasant. In -ieᶜ the muscles of utterance jerk upwards. Melieh must be conceived of by the Englishman as Melié-ăhhh, with long con-

tinued wheezing; and Cerieh as Ceriehi, with final *i* pronounced very rapidly.

27. The true sound of θ and ᴅ, as explained above, is retained at Bagdad in familiar talk; also by the Bedouins, and in reading the Koran or poetry. No one can be misunderstood when he adheres to the correct sounds; and they are so easy to an Englishman, that he ought from the beginning to be punctiliously accurate. To corrupt θ into *s* or *t*, ᴅ into *z* or *d*, confuses words essentially different, and is a really mischievous depravation of the language, though systematically practised by many even of the learned. To merge English *thin* into *tin* or *sin*, *breathe* into *breeze* or *breed*, is just the corruption here deprecated.

28. Double consonants followed by a vowel must be dwelt on, as in Italian *terra, bella*. An Englishman is apt to neglect, and indeed not to understand this. Yet we have it in *meanness, soulless*, which we should never pronounce *meaness, souless;* nor do we confound *nice size* with *nice eyes*, but we sound double *s* in the middle of the former. Only at the end of a word a double consonant cannot be uttered. It remains double for mere grammatical reasons; as Modd (extend).

29. The combination *nb* is properly sounded *mb*, as in Zenbiel (basket), pronounced Zembiel. Its plural is Zenâbiel, where *n* reappears. [In Syria I used to hear Jan'b, Jen'bi, as if with a short vowel elided, instead of Jambi (at my side). This is perhaps comparable to provincial English umb*i*rella, mush*a*room.]

30. The combinations dt, ᴅt, Ẋt, θt, ᵀt, are all sounded as tt: but for grammatical reasons they are not so written.

§ 3. RELATION OF VOWELS TO CONSONANTS.

31. Vowels are of three classes, which (imitating native grammars) I call Fathites, Kisrites, Dhammites. They are thus arranged:

		Short.	Long.
Fathites	Fine Coarse	e a	$\hat{e}=e^z$ $\hat{a}=a^z$
Kisrites	Fine Coarse	i u	ie=iy ui=uy
Dhammites	Fine Coarse	o ö	ou=ow öu=öw

SPECIAL DIPHTHONGS.

Fine	ei=ey	eu=ew
Coarse	ai=ay	au=aw

There is no *grammatical* difference between a *fine* and its corresponding *coarse* vowel or diphthong. The choice between the two is determined by the nature of the contiguous consonants. *Hence even in pointed Arabic they are not distinguished.* [Short *e* or *a* is called Fatha, short *i* or *u* Kisra, short *o* or *ö* Δamma.] One general rule must guide us. *There is a close affinity between the coarse consonants and the coarse vowel-sounds.* Even so, the rule holds but imperfectly of Q, which only with Fathites and diphthongs takes the coarse sounds.

Learned grammars do not always lay stress on the double sound of the vowels, if they name it. Oberleitner, indeed, says (§ 4, 3): "The vowels have a double sound, emphatic with the emphatic consonants, soft with the other letters. *This double sound in practical utterance needs peculiar care, lest words unlike in sense be confounded.*" Caussin de Perceval, in his short but valuable modern grammar, lays chief stress on the difference of *a, á* from *e, é*. Of the rest he says merely, "The guttural and emphatic letters give to the vowels a vague sound which we cannot express by our vowels."

32. To a foreigner the Arab consonants are so difficult, that unless he anxiously attends to the accompanying vowels he has a poor chance of avoiding ridiculous ambiguities. Vowels are more easily heard than consonants; and if we sound them rightly our errors in the consonants will often escape the ear. Hence to *write* this distinction of vowels, and let it impress imagination and memory, is to us of first importance. Even before the same consonant *n* the Arabs say Ana (I), Entè (thou), though they write the first vowel of each word alike. Every European writes A in the former word, E in the latter. Also Man? (who?) is sounded with the vowel of our *bun, none, run*. In regard to the *neutral* consonants there is great uncertainty whether the coarse or the fine vowels are to be used. Even concerning Q before the Kisrites I have more than once changed my opinion. I have asked a person to pronounce to me the word شَمْس (Sun), and have been quite unable to ascertain whether Xams or Xems better denoted his utterance; for he appeared to go backward and forward between the two, or to express something intermediate. So,

whether Θαλᾶθα or Θελέθε be better, may be differently decided at Bagdad and at Beirout.

33. The fine or feminine consonants have a decided preference for the fine vowel sounds; but they are sometimes overpowered by the proximity of a coarse consonant. It is laid down that in WasaT (middle), SaTH (flat roof), the T not merely imposes *a* (instead of *e*) on each word, but changes the sound of *s* (or allows it to be changed) into Ϡ; so that WaϠaT, ϠaTH are a legitimate pronunciation. [So the Latin sounded scriptus for scribtus, optineo for obtineo.] Sometimes it affects orthography, ϠuqTa for SiqTa, hailstone. In a doubtful choice, as, between Bait and Beit (dwelling, lodging) the soft *t* seems a reason for preferring Beit, as in Syria. [Faris directs us to say Bait; but he also bid us say Al, Anta, Jabal, Tall, Malic, Madiena; which every European hears as El, Ente, Jebal, Tell, Melic, Mediena.]

34. Immense ambiguities result from negligence of pronunciation as to coarse and fine sounds. Contrast—

Fitna, sedition;	FuTna, prudence.
Sêr, he proceeded;	Ϡâr, he has become.
Tebaî, he followed;	Tabaî, he printed.
Seif, a sword;	Ϡaif, summer.
SeuT, a whip;	ϠauT, a voice.
Silâh, arms;	Ϡulâh, pacification.
Semm, poison;	Ϡamm, was deaf.
Têb, repented;	Tâb, was nice.
Terec, he left;	Taraq, he knocked.
Cêl, he measured;	Qâl, he said.
Cês, cup;	Qâs, he measured.
Sehil, easy;	Sêhul, seacoast.

Ficr, thought; Faqr, poverty.
Hedd, he demolished; Ḥadd, a limit.
Herab, he fled; Ḥarb, war.
Cewi, he branded; Qawi, strong.
ʿemal, he hoped; Ṭamal, he worked.

So as to difference of mere vowel:

Dohn, grease; Dahin, greasy.
Xoub, dilute; Xaub, sultriness.
Nour, lustre; Naur, a blossom.
Dain, a debt; Dien, (the) faith.
Ḥarr, heat; Ḥörr, free, well-born.
Ṭufl, a young child; Ṭafal, potter's clay.
Ṭajal, haste; Ṭajil, urgent; Ṭujl, calf.
Dibb, creep; Dobb, a bear.

If the Arabs ever have new intercourse with the foreigner, with renewed cultivation and increased refinement, it is probable that their harsh consonants will be greatly softened. A day may come when the words Ṭuin (clay), Tien (figs), will be distinguished by the vowels alone, as Loam and Loom in English. It is truly strange that a system of writing, which (at its best) makes no effort to distinguish such vowel differences, should be imagined perfect.

35. Hebrew is believed by Gesenius to have had fundamentally the same triple distinction of vowels as Arabic; but when the Masoretes analyzed the pronunciation more carefully, they greatly increased the number of vowel marks.

In English some consonants change the sound of vowels. W alters the sound of *a* to *o* in wasp, what, watch, warp, wander, etc. R after *e, i, u, ai, ea, ä,* often changes their sounds. O between *w* and *r* takes the same sound as *e*, *i*, *u*. Such phenomena may aid an Englishman to understand how Arab consonants may modify the vowels.

36. Of the neutral consonants *d* has a special affinity for *a* rather than *e*: the same is sometimes visible of *n*, *b*, *j*. Thus we have (with sound as in English Dumb) Dam' (blood) not Dem; Bann (coffee bean) not Benn; Dâbbe (beast)* not Dêbbe; Jabb (an open well) not Jebb; Janb (a side) not Jenb. When natives *write* these distinctions of vowels they may elicit some general laws at present unknown. Yet it may be safely laid down that R, K, Γ, in common with Q, have an affinity for the coarse Fathites (*a*, *â*) and for the coarse Diphthongs (*ai*, *au*). With these exceptions, the neutral consonants incline to the fine vowel sounds; and none of them ever assume *ö*, *öu*, *ui*. We might add *u*, but for the Syrian pronunciation Cutob, Fulfol, etc., mentioned above in Art. 10. I also used to hear Jufn (eyelid); for which Freytag has Jefn, Jifn, Jofn, as if labouring in vain to express the sound.

37. W, y, ', are called weak consonants, and the other twenty-five, strong. When a weak consonant closes a syllable, it is sometimes dropped, and may be denoted by the apostrophe, as Rama' (he threw) for Ramay. [Catafago usefully introduced this apostrophe.] But generally the weak consonant coalesces with the vowel! thus *a'*, *e'* become *â*, *ê*, and *i'* (which is rare) is sounded *ie*. Thus Mi'ya (a hundred) = Mieya = Miyya. But *aw*, *ew*, *ay*, *ey*, are identical with the diphthongs *au*, *ei*, *ai*, *ei*.

* The *â* is shortened into *a* before the double consonant. This is a general rule. It is written *â*, not *a*, for grammatical reasons.

§ 4. THE PROCESS OF TRANSLITERATION.

38. Rules for transliteration are here given; yet their application should be judiciously postponed, until some familiarity with words has been gained. Those words and combinations with which the pupil is already well acquainted should alone be written in Arabic character.

The European text has first to be prepared by the following modifications. Since the Arabs do not *write* the distinction of fine and coarse vowels, we must throw that distinction away. Hence—

(1) Change *au, eu* to *aw; ou, ōu* to *ow;*
ai, ei to *ay; ie, ui* to *iy;*
also *a' e'* to *ay; iá, uá* to *iyá;*
final *i* to *iy; iey* to *iyy; ia* to *iya.*

(2) Final *a, e*, which is a feminine termination, <u>may</u> be dotted to represent ّ (dotted *h*).

Observe that *a, i, o* (the only short vowels then remaining), are to be expressed by a vowel point (FatHa, Kisra, Xamma) attached to the *preceding letter*. If no letter precede (*i.e.* if the *a, i, o* begin the word), Elif must be written, *to carry the vowel point*. FatHa is *over* the letter, Kisra *under* it, but of the same form; as ن na; ن ni. Xamma (*o*) is a comma *over* the letter; as ن no. Circumflexed *á, é*, in general are denoted by Elif ا with FatHa over the *preceding* letter; but at the beginning of a word the Elif receives instead a circumflex to lengthen it, آ.

After adding Elif thus to all words that need it, incorporate the particles Wa, Fa, La, E, the article El, and the prepositions Bi, Ce, Li, with the word following; every European consonant being expressed (from the Table in the Frontispiece) by the corresponding Arabic consonant. The learner will perhaps at first make errors about Elif, which alone is anomalous.

The particles Ma, ⵍe (of Hêⵍe) have Elif (ا) for a final letter. In a few words (as Allâh, God; Lêcin, but; Hêⵍe, this; Ⲑelêⲑ, three), the Elif for *á*, *ê*, is irregularly omitted in Arabic text. Final *h* dotted (ة) is written for feminine *-a*, *-e*, or *-at*, *-et*, final. But to every plural verb of 3rd pers. ending in *ou*, Elif is arbitrarily added.

Lastly, the adverbial termination *-an*, *-en*, is not to be denoted by ں in the text, but by اً with double Fatḥa.

39. For the actual junction of the Arabic letters, a few details will be useful. The *order* of the letters in a word is the reverse of English; viz., from right to left. The letters د, ذ, ر, ز, و, ا, are never joined to one following, hence they remain nearly unchanged (except when دﺵ are sometimes combined). Elif is joined at the bottom to a letter before it, as بﺎ *bá*; and Lam-Elif (*lá*) has the form لا or لا.

Most of the consonants end with a flourish, which has to be cut off in junction: thus ح becomes ﺣ. Initial *h* is written ه, but *h* joined at each side is ﻬ. M in the middle of a word is a loop falling below the line. ⲣ (Ain) joined on both sides is ﻌ; joined on one side, it is ﻋ when initial and ﻊ when final. The letters ج, ح, خ, require that a letter preceding shall *mount above them*; hence it becomes sometimes uncertain to which a dot belongs. When *l* is followed by *m*, the loop of *m* is generally thrown out to the right, as لم (*lm*). A double consonant is not written twice in the text, but receives a mark like *w* over it, called *textied*. The same mark is placed over *l* of the article El, when it is assimilated to the consonant following. Thus Ommi is أُمِّي, Omem is أُمَم, El xams is اَلشَّمْس.

It is a good rule, extensively used, to retain the two dots under ي (*y*) at the end of a word, when the *y* is sounded, and omit the dots when the *y* is mute; which is here written *a'*, *e'*.

It remains at option to omit all the vowel points.

Expertness in any new type can only be earned by practice. The learner may get partial help from the words in a later section, written in alternate type.

PART II.—ON GRAMMAR.

§ 1. NOUNS AND ADJECTIVES.

1. GENDER OF NOUNS.—Arabic Nouns are masculine or feminine, often arbitrarily. *a.* Names of things female are naturally feminine. *b.* So are names of countries, towns, and villages. *c.* So are the names of the double members of the body, as Yed, hand; Rijl, foot. *d.* So are the collective nouns technically called broken plurals. *e.* So are most nouns ending in *á, é, a', e', a, e:* as, Ṭa'ṣâ, a staff; Cisê, garment; Marse', harbour; Milhe', musical instrument; Mediena, city; Mélice, queen.

Feminines in *a, e,* have lost *t* from the end. Those in *a', e',* have generally lost *y*, and those in *á, é,* sometimes *w*, sometimes ʽ. In certain inflexions they regain their lost consonant.

2. The feminine of a noun is sometimes formed from the masculine by adding *a* or *e ;* as Celb, a dog; *f.* Celbe, Celba: Ṭamm, father's brother, Ṭamma, father's sister; Kâl, mother's brother, Kâla, mother's sister; Jadd, grandfather, Jadda, grandmother. But for the commonest relations and nobler animals the feminine has an independent name; as Ḥuṣân, horse, Faras, mare; ʽEsed, lion, Lebouʽa, lioness. [The

female horse being commoner than the male, the Arabs say "mare" when the sex is not thought of: as, "Have you no mare to ride?" We similarly say cows, sheep; not bulls, rams. To define the feminine idea Mare, if error be feared, the diminutive Foraise (filly), says Kazimirski, is used for Mare.]

3. The ADJECTIVE follows its noun, and agrees with it in gender. Its feminine is ordinarily formed by adding *a, e*.

> Rajol qawi, a strong man.
> Mar²a jamiel*e*, a beautiful woman.
> Ṣabi semien, a fat boy.
> Darb wesik(*a*), a dirty road.
> Melic jaliel, a majestic king.
> Bint Ṣaḥier*a*, a little girl.
> Jâriya naḥuil*e*, a slender damsel.
> Dâr fasiḥ*a*, a spacious house.
> Celb mouʌi, a troublesome dog.
> Melice jaliel*e*, a majestic queen.

[Mar²a, woman, is classical, and is the only word that I heard from the people. (Do not confound it with Marra, "a single time," *une fois*.) In modern prose, the learned appear always to write Imrâ²a, a woman.]

Some adjectives end in *i* (unaccented) which is shortened from *iey*, as Qáwi, strong, for Qawiey; Ingliezi, English, for Inglicziey. In the feminine the accent falls on this syllable, and the *y* comes back; as Qawiéya, Inglicziéya.

Adjectives of the type Ṣabour (patient) do not form any special feminine, nor do those which naturally have no masculine; as Ḥâmil, Ḥâbil, pregnant.

Some verbal adjectives in *ân* change the termination into *a'* for the feminine; as Secrân, drunken, *f.* Secra'.

Adjectives of the type Akras, Axheb, will be mentioned in Art. 12; and Comparatives in 95-97.

4. For convenience of *reference* two lists of Nouns are here given, the gender of which could not be guessed by their sense or type.

The following are feminine:—

Age, sinn*	Liver, cibad
Axe, faˁs	Machine, manjanieq
Barley, xaʈuir	Oath, yemien
(Broad) Beans, foul	Park, firdaus
Bow, qaus	Paunch, ⎫
Bucket of leather, dalou	Lobe, ⎬ cirx
Buttock, ist	Ventricle, ⎭
Cup, ceˁs	Razor, mous
Cuirass, dirʈ	Scorpion, ʈaqrab
Earth, ˁerẔ	Salt, milḥ
Finger, uʃbaʈ	Self, Soul, nefs
Fire, nâr	Sole, ⎫ naʈl
Fox, θeʈlab	Horseshoe, ⎭
Gold, ᴧcheb	Spider, ʈancebout
Hare, arnab	Sun, xams
Hell, jaḥuim	Trowser, xarwâl
—— jehennam	War, ḥarb
House, dâr	Well, biˁr
Hyena, ẕabʈ	Wind, rieḥ
Left-hand, ximâl	Wine, kamr.

* Sinn, properly means *Tooth*.

The following are of either gender:—

Arms, silâḣ	Peace, selm
Authority, solṪân	——— Ṡolḣ
Cutlas, kanjar	Road, darb
(Full) Day, Ⱦöḣaʾ	Soil, Mould, θeraʾ
Heaven, semâʿ	State, Ḣâl
Knife, siccien	Stewpot, qidr
Musk, misc	Tongue, lisên
Nape, qifâ	Way, Ṫarieq
Neck, Ṫönq	Womb, raḣum.
Path, sebiel	

5. DUAL OF NOUNS.—All nouns form a regular dual. [In Barbary only names of things naturally double. This is as Hebrew.] The classical dual has two cases—absolute case in *án, én;* oblique case in *ain, ein;* but in conversation the absolute is never heard. Feminines that have lost *t, w, y,* resume it in the dual. Indeed, those in *aʾ, eʾ,* are treated as if they had *always* lost *y,* and those in *á, é,* as if they had lost *w.* Thus:

Rajol-ein, two men	Jebal-ein, two mountains
Marʿat-ein, two women	Medienat-ein, two cities
Melic-ein, two kings	Yed-ain, two hands
Melicʾt-ein,* two queens	Rijl-ein, two feet
Fetey-ein, two lads, two young men	Milhey-ein, two musical instruments
ṪaṠaw-ain, two staffs	Ridaw-ain, two mantles
Marsey-ein, two harbours	Cisew-ein, two garments.

6. The PLURALS of Nouns and Adjectives are generally Imperfect and irregular: as Xaiʿ, a thing, *pl.* Axyâʿ, things;

* Or Melʾcetein.

Insên, a human being, *pl.* Nês, men, Nisê or Niswân, women; Celb, a dog; Cilâb, dogs. Most of what are called plurals are collective nouns feminine; as, in English, from a Steed comes a Stud, from Cord, Cordage.

One form of Imperfect plural looks like a classical dual, but has a vowel change in the penultima; as Nâr, fire; Nierân, fires. I propose to call this the False Dual. The topic of the imperfect plurals must be postponed.

7. PERFECT PLURALS.—Most feminine nouns in *a', e', â, é*, make a real or perfect plural in *ât, ét;* so do many feminines in *a, e;* especially when formed from a masculine. Thus from Melic, *f.* Melice, queen, *pl.* Melicêt, queens; from Bafl, *f.* Bafala, *pl.* Bafalât, female mules. Almost the only masculine nouns which make a perfect plural are those which denote tradesmen. These are of the form Kabbâz, baker; Baqqâl, greengrocer. The nominative ought to be in *oun;* but popularly *ien* serves for all cases; as Kabbâzien, bakers.

8. ARTICLE.—El, the, is indeclinable, and precedes its noun. Before fourteen consonants, fancifully termed Lunar, El retains its full pronunciation. But before x, s, z, š, ž, r, t, θ, d, ð, T, ▵, n (which, with l, are called Solar), l by an unfortunate slovenly pronunciation takes the sound of the consonant following, and is popularly lost to the ear. Thus, El dien, the faith, is sounded Ed dien. I put a zero under *l* to mark this change. [The printer is forced at present to use a *dot* for a *zero.*] Thus:

El̥ xams, the sun   But El qamar, the moon
El̥ dâr, the house   El beit, the dwelling
El̥ ra's, the head   El melic, the king
El̥ darb, the road   El celb, the dog.

The obliteration of the sound of *l*, which has invaded half of the Arabic, is universal in Hebrew. [Whether the likeness of El to Latin Ille be accidental, is curious matter for inquiry. Compare Olâ, these, Δê-l-ic, that yonder; Art. 28 below.]

El in some combinations means *this*; as Elycum, to-day; El⁵en, (at) this season, now; Elsêʿa, this instant. In such words I write it as in composition.

Our *indefinite* article A, An, is understood without expression.

9. The article El must be added to the adjective as well as to the noun; as, El rájol el ʿtawiel, the tall man. Before the adjective it then differs little from a relative pronoun; "*the* man *who* (is) tall." Feminine *a* of the noun regains its *t* before El.

> El nehr el aʿsfar, the yellow river.
> El jâriyat el jamiele, the beautiful damsel.
> El jébal el xâmik, the lofty mountain.
> El doroub el wésika, the dirty roads.
> El ʿtaʿtâm el ʿtaiyib, the nice food.
> El celb el xáris, the illnatured dog.
> El dâr el cebiera, the great house.
> El cilâb el mouΔiya, the mischievous dogs.

Occasionally a foreign adjective precedes its noun. Thus (Bagdad) *keux* beit, a *good* house. Especially in Turkish titles, as, El *bâx* qawwâs, the *chief* bowman. Then El is not repeated.

A small number of substantives are current in the sense of adjectives, and these always precede the noun. The most important to be here named, are, Coll, Jamieʿt, all; Cilê, both; Souʳ, ill, evil; Ṭair, other. Thus, Souʳ kabar, ill news, bad news; Souʳ bakt, ill luck; Ṭair xaiʳ, another thing, *i.e.*, quite a different affair. The opposite phrase is, Farad xaiʳ, one thing, a single thing, *i.e.*, it is all one, it comes to the same, it does not matter. [In Bagdad they say, Farad baſl, "*a* mule." But this is degenerate style.]

10. There is a type called the NOUN OF UNITY, which is often derived from a noun expressing a material, fruit, or small animals collectively. The type is simply that of a feminine in -*a*, -*e*. Thus:

>Kobz, bread; Kobze, a bit of bread.
>Laḧm, meat; Laḧma, a piece of meat.
>Semn, butter; Semne, a piece of butter.
>Zebieb, raisins; Zebiebe, a raisin.
>Ṭúnab, grapes; Ṭúnaba, a grape.
>Xájar, trees; Xájara, a tree.
>Naml, ants; Namle, an ant.
>Ṭöub, brick; Ṭöuba, a brick.
>Maṭz, goats; Maṭze, a goat.

Arabic has many collective nouns, as Kail, horses; Ibl, camels; Maṭz, goats; Baqar, oxen; Ẋân, sheep; Mehê, deer; Ṭair, birds. But they do not always yield a noun of unity. Dictionaries tell us that Baqara is noun of unity, and means an ox as well as a cow; but the people seem to use Baqara solely for a cow, which has no other specific name. N.B.— Since we can say El kobze, *the* piece of bread, the noun of unity only suggests A, An accidentally, but does not express it.

11. If the article is expressed before the substantive, but

omitted before the adjective, the adjective becomes a predicate, and *is* or *are* is understood. (Mixed examples:)

El ḥarr el xadied,
   the intense heat.
El jebal xâmik,
   the mountain *is* lofty.
El xajarat el xâmiqa,
   the lofty tree.
El ceᶻs fâƛua,
   the cup (glass) *is* empty.
El soccer Taiyib,
   the sugar *is* nice.
El leil el bârid,
   the cold night.
El bâb meftouḥ,
   the door *is* open.
El xehr el qâbil,
   the approaching month.
El leil moƛlim,
   the night is dark.
El ᶻemr el mohimm,
   the important affair.
El xaiᶻ mofimm,
   the thing *is* vexatious.
Axyâᶻ ḥaqiera,
   petty matters.
ᶻEmr Saʕb,
   a difficult (grievous) affair.
El ᶻemr el Saʕb,
   the grievous affair.

El zemân Tawiel,
   the time *is* long.
El rajol najjâr,
   the man *is* a carpenter.
El aulâd mouᴀia,
   the children *are* mischievous.
El héwâ bârid,
   the air *is* cold.
El qadaḥ el fârif,
   the empty goblet.
El kâdim ḥâƛur,
   the servant *is* ready.
El darb Tawiel(e),
   the road *is* long.
El Tarieq el ʕâmma,
   the public way.
El belad baʕuid,
   the district *is* distant.
El cilâb wesika,
   the dogs *are* dirty.
El ḥaiT el semiec,
   the thick wall.
El xabbêc moseccer,
   the window *is* shut.
El rieḥ xadieda,
   the wind *is* intense.
Jihêd ʕaʒuim,
   a mighty enterprize.

12. The following list of adjectives may be convenient:—

Great, cebier
Small, ṣaſier
Mighty, ʕaẓuim
Petty, ḥaqier
Much, ccθier (Many)
Little, qaliel (Few)
Long, ṭawiel (Tall)
Short, qaʃuir
High, ʕâli
Low, wâṭu
Broad, ʕarieᶁ
Narrow, ᶁaiyiq
Wide, wesieʕ
Deep, ʕamieq
Shallow, xâyif (Catafago)
Thick, semiec
Thin, raqieq
Fat, semien
Lean, naḥuif
Heavy, θeqiel
Light, kafief
Strong, qáwiey
Weak, ᶁaʕuif
Intense, xadied
Gentle, laʕuif
Hard, (stiff, cruel) qâsi
Soft, laiyin
Sharp, ḥâdd
Blunt, cêll

Quick, serieʕ
Slow, bâṭu
Hot, sokn, ḥârr
Cold, bârid (bardân)
Warm, dâfi (dafyân)
Tepid, fêtir
Wet, mabloul
Moist, raṭub
Dry, yâbis
—— nâxif
Clean, naᶁuif (ظ).
Dirty, wésik
Nice, ṭaiyib
Nasty, cerieh
Salt, mâliḥ
Bitter, morr
Sweet, (dulcis) ḥölou
—— (suavis) ʕáᶑib
Sour, ḥâmuᶁ
Acid, ḥâmiz
Full, melˀân
Empty, fâriſ
Dear, ſâli
Cheap, rakieʃ
Valuable, nefies
Worthless, ʕúfax (rubbish)
Good, melieḥ
Bad, rádiey
Better, aḥsen

Excellent, jaiyid	Happy, seƮuid
Vile, ra⌃iel	Wretched, mescien
Useful, nâfuƮ	Hale, Ʈâfi
Useless, bâƮul	Sick, marieẊ
Noble, najieb	Rich, ſániey
Vulgar, hemjiey	Poor, faqier
Superior (in quality), rafieƮ	Near, qarieb
	Distant, baƮuid
Inferior, dániey	Ancient, qadiem
Wise, Ʈâqil	Old (thing), Ʈatieq
Stupid, belied	New, jadied
Learned, Ʈâlim	Difficult, painful, ꝣaƮb
Ignorant, jêhil	Easy, sehil
Skilful, mêhir	Arduous, Ʈasier
Clumsy, ſaxiem	Slight, heiyin.

To these we must add a few remarkable adjectives of the type Axheb, which express the primary *colours* or bodily *defects*.

Red, aḦmar	Blue, ezraq
Green, akẊar	Grey, axheb
Yellow, aꝣfar	White, abyaẊ
Brown, esmar	Black, eswad.
Blind, aƮma'	Left-handed, axwal
One-eyed, aƮwar.	Born lame, aƮraj
Deaf, aƮrax	Bald, aꝣlaƮ
Dumb, akras	Leprous, abraꝣ.

They are declined as AḦmar, red; *f.* Ḧamrâ; *pl.* Ḧömr;

only that the plural of Abyaȝ, white, is Buiȝ, by a law of euphony, for Boyȝ.

The *substantives* expressing colour, derived from the above, are Ħömra, Koȝra, Ȝöfra, Somra, Zorqa, Xohba, Biyâȝ, Sewâd(a). Examples:

Eļ semawât ħamrâ,	El qamar abyaȝ,
the heavens (are) red.	the moon (is) white.
El ſoyoum seudâ,	El Ingliez buiȝ,
the clouds (are) black.	the English (are) white.
Eļ dənyâ zerqâ,	Eļ raml esmar,
the world (sky) is blue.	the sand (is) brown.
El kail zorq,	El biſâl somr,
the horses (are) blue (*i.e.* grey!)	the mules (are) brown.

13. It is impossible to examine these lists of adjectives without being struck by their forms. Such as Cebier, Ceθier, Xadied, differ in the three consonants only, but have the same vowels. In these we regard the root (or characteristic part) to be Cbr, Cθr, Xdd; and in fact, most words of the language are thus referable to *three radical* letters. But it is well here to enumerate the chief types of adjectives:

1. The type Sehil, level; Semij, gross, rank; Nehim, ravenous; Ħamiz, acid.
2. Bârid, cold; Ħâmuȝ, sour; Ħâmiz, acid; Ģâli(y), dear; Fêtir, lukewarm. (This is an active participle or participial adjective.)
3. Ṭanied, obstinate; Melich, fair, fine, good; ʿEnieq, agreeable; Xarier, evil. This is on the whole the commonest type. (Only when *w* or *y* is the second radical, *w* is assimilated to *y*, and transposition takes place; as Ṭaiyib,

nice; Laiyin, soft for Ṭayieb, Layien; Heiyin, slight, easy, for Hewien.)

4. Ḣasoud, envious; Ṭamoul, active; Raḣoum, merciful. (This type denotes *fulness*, as our termination *-ful* and Latin *-osus*.)

5. Xaṣṣâl, busy, devoted to business; Meccêr, swindler. (This type denotes *habit*, and is very common to express tradesmen; as Najjâr, carpenter.)

6. Aḣmaq, fatuous; Esmar, black; Akras, dumb; were treated in Art. 12.

7. Xirrier, villainous; Siccier, very drunken. (This expresses *energy*. In the classical language there are several other types for energy.)

8. Bardân, sensible of cold; Jauṭân, hungry; Ṭaʿtxân, thirsty; Teṭbân, weary; Melʾên, full; Dafyân, sensible of warmth.

9. Adjectives of *relation* end in *-iey*; as Hemjiey, vulgar, from Hemj, populace.

10. Various participles are formed by initial M, which must be afterwards classified.

Of these the two most important have the types:

a. Maʿtloum, known; Maxfoul, busied, busy; MeΔcour, aforenamed; Makʿṣöuʿṣ, peculiar, proper.

b. Motṭub, tiresome; MouΔi(y), mischievous; Moθmin, costly; Moθmir, fruitful: in which head we include Moʿimm, vexatious (for Moʿmim); Mohieb, frightful (for Mohyib).

Ṣaʿib, difficult; Waʿtr, rugged; exhibit the first type in a ruder state, in which (as in English) *participle* and *gerund* are confounded. (For there is no commoner type of the of the gerund, *i.e.* of the verbal noun of action.) In fact, the language exhibits Sehil or Sehl, level, easy; Waʿtur or

Waîr, rugged; Ṱaʌib or Ṱaʌb, sweet (water) without discrimination.

Obs. 1.—The adjective of relation has no fixed *type*, only a fixed *termination:* for it adds *-iey* to a noun of any type whatever. Thus, from Melc, a king, *pl.* Molouc, we have both Melciey and Moluciey, royal, regal.

Obs. 2.—The Western learner needs peculiar vigilance in regard to the sense of Arabic adjectives. Our adjectives habitually take two senses active and passive (sometimes more), even in the flattest prose, without our being aware of anything figurative. Thus we say, a wise man, a wise law; he was doubtful; a doubtful question; but the Arabs, saying Rajol Ṱâqil, a wise man; would on no account make Ṱâqil the epithet of a law; but Maṱqoul, (made wisely?) will do. So a man who is doubtful, *i.e.* who doubts, is Xêcic; but a doubtful question is Maxcouc. In these examples the Arabs in fact use active and passive participles.

14. An adjective may be followed by a COMPLEMENTARY NOUN, which is adverbial in use. The noun is either preceded by El, or takes -an, -en, (the Adverbial Case, Art. 158) as its inflection. This is similar to the idiom familiar in Greek and Latin (as, *Os humerosque* Deo similis), where we supply *as to,* or some equivalent preposition, *in, of.* In classical Arab style this idiom abounds to satiety.

Cebier el Ṱômr,
    great of age.
Ḣasen el Ṡoura,
    handsome of figure.
Ḣadd el Ṱaraf,
    sharp at the end.

Ṱawiel el ajniḣa,
    long in the wings.
Ṱaʒuim qowwaten,
    mighty in strength.
Ṱadiem el raḣma,
    void of mercy.

Ei ʰesed! Ƭaʒuim el kalqa, mohieb eḷ ʒoura, mokawwif el
   fâyila.
What a lion! mighty of build, frightful of figure, formidable
   of onset.

15. An adverb should properly follow the adjective which
it modifies, or the adjective with its complement; as,

Aʒfar jiddan,	Ƭawiel ceθieran,
yellow very.	long in excess, too tall.
Cebier el Ƭömr jiddan,	Semicc xaiʰen,
old very.	somewhat thick.

Many adverbs (derived from noun or adjective) end in -*an*
or -*ten;* but in vulgar Arabic this termination is often dropped,
and the adverb precedes the adjective. Thus at Aleppo,
Qáwi melieḧ (*fort* bon), "very good," for Melieḧ jiddan.
Ana xowaiya marieẌ, "I am a wee-bit ill," for Ana marieẌ
xaiʰen, I am somewhat ill. But this may be called slang.

Peculiar attention is in this stage due to Jiddan, very;
Xaiʰen, somewhat; Ceθieran, much, too much; Qalielan,
scantily, but little, a little; FaqaƬ, only (for which vulgarly
Bes in Syria); and Ɣair, not (*before an adjective*); as Ɣair
melieḧ, not good; Ɣair ràẌu, displeased; Ɣair Ƭaiyib,
unpleasant.

Kobz faqaƬ,	Eḷ darb ɣair Ƭawiele,
bread only.	the road *is* not long.
Kobz qaliel faqaƬ,	El ʰemr ʒaƭb xaiʰen,
a little bread only.	the affair *is* somewhat difficult
El mecên ɣair qarieb,	El ʰomour ɣair ʒaƭba,
the place *is* not near.	the affairs *are* not difficult.

§ 2. COMPOSITE STATE OF NOUNS.

16. (*Status constructus*). The English combine two nouns, as Sea-side, Gold-watch, so as to make the former a virtual adjective. The Arabs do the same thing in principle: only, as their adjective *follows* its noun, it is the latter of the two which they make adjectival. Thus from Kaziena, treasury, and Auràq, leaves, papers, they make Auràq-kaziena, treasury-scrip.

The order being the reverse to that of English, we imagine the word *of* between the two nouns, as Scrip (of) treasury. The particle *of* is wanting to the Arabs; yet they have several modes of supplying it, which will be afterwards stated.

17. When either noun is left *indefinite*, one may generally hear between them the vowel *a* or *e;* as Auràq-a-kaziena. So: Kaix-a-xaîr, cloth (of) hair, *i.e.* sackcloth; Tekt-e-melic, throne (of a) king; Jild-a-jâmous, leather (of) buffalo. In fact, it is often hard to utter the words without some vowel of union. Nor only so, but a vowel (whether *a*, *i*, or *o*) *is here strictly classical;* though *i* is objectionable to the vulgar as seeming to mean *my*, and *o* as seeming to mean *his*. To write *a* or *e* here seems irreprovable; but that it is necessary cannot be pretended. This intermediate vowel, if we write it, will be comparable to *t* in French *A-t-il*, which has come out of the Latin *Habet ille*.

If we desire to mark strongly that the second noun is indefinite, we may insert before it, Wâhud, a certain; as Citêb wâhud qasies, a book of a certain priest. N.B.—Wâhud *after* its noun, is the emphatic numeral, One, *unus*, a single; as Qasies wâhud, one priest. Before the noun, it is less emphatic and answers to *quidam*, a certain.

18. Much oftener, the nouns are both defined; then El joins them, and applies to both; as, Jild-el-jâmous, *the* hide (of) *the* buffalo. Here El *seems* to mean Of, nearly as in Art. 14, where it was joined to a complementary noun.

Some compounds have become fixed, as though single words: thus Ra's-e-mâl, capital (in trade); or Resmâl: literally *caput rei*, head (of) property: also Qillet-el-bakt, deficiency of luck, *i.e.* ill luck. Compare such fixed phrases as Man-of-war; Aid-de-camp, in Western tongues.

19. More examples:

Sebab el moʃuiba,
  the cause of the disaster.
Wofour el aflâl,
  the abundance of the crops.
Aurâq el kaziena,
  the scrip of the treasury.
'Omour el memlece,
  the affairs of the kingdom.
Awâmir el melic,
  the commands of the king.
Makzen têjir,
  a warehouse of a merchant.
Makzen el têjir,
the warehouse of the merchant.
Joloud woɦöux,
  skins of wild animals.

Aurâq el xajara,
  the leaves of the tree.
Dar el jinân (*Paradise*),
  the house of the gardens.
Serier el solʈân,
  the throne of the sultan.
'Emier elâi (*Colonel*),
  prince of a regiment.
Bafl el qasies,
  the mule of the priest.
Bafl wâɦud qasies,
  a mule of a certain priest.
Qiʃâʃ el jinâya,
  the punishment of the offence.
Nâʒur el mâlia,
  the overseer of finance.

20. If the former of two nouns in composition be a feminine in -*a*, -*e*, it resumes (or may resume) its lost *t* in composition; as, Rixâqa, agility; but, Rixâqat el ʈasêcir, the

agility of the soldiery. This is undoubtedly the classical and the very ancient method; in fact it is Hebrew, where the feminine in -*ah*, changes into -*at* in like case. The Arabs also surmount their *h* (ѕ) with the two dots of their *t;* which proves the idiom to be older than the present orthography; for if those who fixed it had sounded the *t* in *all* relations of the noun, they would have represented it by an ordinary *t*. Thus the *t* should not be always sounded,—perhaps *only before the article* El, or *before another noun in composition*. On the other hand, I found instructors in Aleppo to differ much, whether *t* should be sounded even in the latter case; and Cherbonneau, Léon, and Hélot are very inconsistent in the matter in their transliterations. But I believe the *t* should always be sounded in these two connections.

Turkish words in â (as Baxâ, Afâ) and a few Arabic words in â, change -*â* into -*at* in composition; as, Bâxat Ḥaleb, Pasha of Aleppo. (Especially Donyâ, world, sky, weather; Jouwa, within; Barra, without,—popular words.)

21. If the second noun in composition be adjectival, obscurity may result; thus, Ibn faqier suggests A poor son; not, A son of a poor (man). To express the latter, we may prefix Rajol (man) or Wâḥud (one) to Faqier; as Ibn-a-rajol-faqier. Only in this position, if the nouns admit an adjective of the same gender and number, it is uncertain to which the adjective belongs. Thus Goṣöun el xajarat el Ṭawiele, is either, The boughs of the tall tree, or, The long boughs of the tree; since the imperfect plural is treated grammatically as a feminine. But:

Kail(-a)-ṭaseer el kafiefa, the light horse of the army.
Rejâ el nês el θébit, the firm hope of the men.

Kazienat el melic el ῾aᴣuim, the treasury of the mighty king.
Majlis eḷ tenᴣuimât el ῾âli, the high Board of Arrangements.
Wocelâ eḷ sel῾anat el fikâm, the august ministers of the empire.
Kazienat el melic el fâᴅua, the empty treasury of the king.

22. When the former noun is a dual, its *n* is elided; thus, Yedain, two hands, Yedai'-fars, the (two) forefeet of a mare; Yedai' el melic, the (two) hands of the king. Jâriyatei' el melice, *the* two damsels of the queen.

23. If an adjectival word can fitly precede its noun (as a superlative may), it equally well precedes a compound: thus, since Awwal yeum (the first day) is correct, so is Awwal yeum-eḷ-sene (the first day-of-the year); though it is equally good to say, Yeum-eḷ-sene el ̣awwal. [On the same principle we read in Loqman's Fables, hêᴅih jorzet el Ḣa῾ab, *this* bundle of wood; although jorzet el Ḣa῾ab hêᴅih, appears to be normal, Art. 33.]

24. Three and even more nouns may be strung together in composition; but only the last can take the article (or a possessive pronoun), and this makes them *all* definite. The first of three is sometimes the numeral One, used pronominally; E᾽Ḣad, *fem.* UḢda'; as:

E᾽Ḣad a῾ᴅâ el majlis, one of the members of the Board.
UḢda' medâyin* el melic, one of the cities of the king.

Also an adjective which agrees with the former noun is often evaded by paraphrase. Thus, for, The kind exertions of the Pasha, they say, The kind*ness of the* exertions of the Pasha; making a triple compound, Ḣösn mesê῾ui el Bâxâ. The kind

* *Or*, modon.

attention of the Right Hon. Fouad Pasha, Ḧösn iltifât Fouâd Bâxâ el moᶜaƷƷam; *lit.* the kindness of the attention, etc.

Serier melic Iᵗâlia, the throne of the King of Italy.

Hoboub riyâḧ eḷ ximâl, the blowing of the winds of the North.

The newspapers carry this concatenation of nouns to an offensive extreme; as, Teᶜalloq eᶜmâl ᵗömoum ehêli ᶜaʃumat el bilâd, The dependence of the hopes of the university of the population of the capital of the country; for, The dependence of the hopes of the whole metropolitan population.

25. CONNECTIVE AND DISJUNCTIVE PARTICLES.

Wa (*vulg.* Ou), and.

Fa, and next; and then; then.

Lêcin, Walêcin, Lecinna (with pronouns), but, but yet.

ᶜEmma, Waᶜemma, Faᶜemma, but, however (cæterum?).

Bel, nay but even: Lat. *at,* or Germ. *sondern.*

Au, or.

Imma—au, either—or.

Imma—ᶜem, whether—or.

Incên—em—au, whether—or—or.

Imma—waᶜilla, either (whether)—or else.

[Catafago has Yâ—yâ, either—or. I find no other authority, and never heard it. Yâ, or, is Persian.]

26. ᴅcheb wa fuᴅᴅa, gold and silver.

Rajol ᵗawiel wa qawi, a man tall and strong.

Imma cebier au ʃafier, either great or little.

Elwân bieᴅ wa soud wa ḧomr wa koᴅr, colours white and black and red and green.

Here the connective particle is repeated oftener than with us, and this is popular. But in careful style they are often fond of mere apposition, as the Latins, disregarding particles of connection. Thus:

Beit Ḣasen, mecien, mottáqin el binâ,
A house handsome, substantial, perfect of building.

Fa has idiomatic uses in which it seems to be redundant, like the English interjection Well! thrown in to gain time for the speaker. It often occurs at the *apodosis* or response, and may be rendered Then.

27. Two nouns united by Wa (and) may form the *second* part of a compound, as:

Ḣösn el Ḣöqoul wa el fiyâẊ,
the beauty of the fields and woods.
Ewâni eḷ ⌃cheb wa el fuẊẊa,
vessels of gold and silver.

But to make such a union the *former* part of a compound (as, Tors wa seif el mediena, the shield and sword *of* the city) is not approved. The standard order is: The shield of the city, and *its* sword, Tors el mediena wa seifohe. (Of the pronoun we shall presently speak.) The necessity of this formula is an unpleasant constraint.

A composite noun may become the complement to an adjective, with the syntax of Art. 14. Thus Faris (Nat. Hist.) has "El jibâl el ceθiera(t) xajar-eḷ-ˁSanauber, the mountains which are plentiful *in* pine trees;" just as we may say, Ceθier eḷ xajar, plentiful *in* trees. But obscurity of syntax accumulates through the barbarous deficiency of the language in this and other small matters.

§ 3. DEMONSTRATIVES AND EMPHATIC PRONOUNS.

28. The demonstratives are three, as Hic, Iste, Ille, in Latin; and originally referred to the three persons, meaning This of *mine* (or, this *here*), That of *thine*, and That of *his* (or, that *yonder*). But the second class naturally abounding most in dialogue has nearly exterminated the third in the spoken language.

The two first classes, except in Africa, are generally compounded with the particle Hè, Lo! behold!

m. △ê, Hè△e, this; △êc, He△êc, that; △êlic, that.
f. △ie, Tie, Hè△ih; △iec, Tiec, Hetiec; Tile.
pl. (Olà), Hê²olâ, these; Olâ²ic, Hê²oláic, those; (Olâlic) those.
adv. Honâ, Hêhonâ, here; Hònêc, there; Honâlic, there yonder.
   Ce△ê, Hêce△ê, so; Ce△êlic, thus, likewise.

Also, pronouns of 3rd person;

| Hou, Houa, he | Hom (Homma), they (*m.*) |
| Hie, Hiya, she | (Hon) Honna, they (*f.*) |

29. One may conjecture that Olà is really the plural of El, which originally may have meant *He* (ille); but Olâ and Olâlic seem to be entirely obsolete. Wright, in his grammar of *ancient* Arabic, says that Olâlic is extremely rare, being supplanted by Olâ²ic. Even △êlic and Tile are called "high style" by Caussin De Perceval; nevertheless they may be heard when strong emphasis is needed. The classical dual *m.* Hè△ein, *f.* Hètein (those two) is understood, but little used. The same is true of the dual Homâ (they two, them two). Besides, there are many variations of local dialect,

with which it may be unwise in this stage to burden a learner. They will be easily picked up on occasion. Those that are here written down cannot be misunderstood, and are classical.

30. Closely akin to the demonstratives is Hêt (hither! bring thou!) which is inflected like an imperative: *m.s.* Hêt; *f.s.* Hêti; *pl.* Hêtou. Faris gives the word in popular conversation, so we may presume that it is popularly understood. Ordinarily one hears Jieb, Jiebi, Jiebou (bring) which is a verb purely modern.

31. Another remarkable demonstrative is △ou, *f.* △êt; *pl.* △ewien, *f. pl.* △ewât. Among the Tay Arabs it is said to serve as the relative Qui. In classical use it is like the Greek article in certain connections with a genitive; as △ewie-hi, τοὺς αὐτοῦ, those who are his. But in general, prefixed to a noun, it means *endowed with*; thus, from Ꞩaql, intellect, △ou Ꞩaql, intelligent. This is at once classsical and popular. The *n* of △ewien naturally vanishes in the composite state; thus, Nês △ewie' Ꞩaql, intelligent men. From Jemâl, beauty, Marʿa △êt jemâl, a beautiful woman. When Ꞩair (Art. 15) is used to express negation before such a compound, it changes △ou to △ie, as Ꞩair △ie Ꞩaql, *not* intelligent. See 157 below.

Very numerous compound adjectives in English are paraphrased in Arabic by help of △ou. Thus, The sharp-headed whale, el fâꞨöus △ou el raʿs el Ḥâdd; The golden-eyed duck, el baꞨꞨ △ou el Ꞩain el △ehebieya. So too our adjectives formed in *-ed* from a noun; as, The crest*ed* duck, el baꞨꞨ △ou el Ꞩörra.

The words Ꞩâhub (companion) and ʿEhl (folk) are astonishingly used to replace ▵ou in this idiom. This appears every way in bad taste and undesirable; yet it exists as a fact.

▵ê, ▵ou, must have a real, though distant, relation to English *The*, which may be traced through Indo-Germanic and Hebræo-African tongues.

32. With a proper name, the demonstrative needs to be thrown behind; as, Istenboul hê▵e, this (city) Constantinople.

Observe,—that Hê▵e rajol means, *this (is) a man*. To express *This man*, we must insert the article between, as in prose Greek; Hê▵e el rajol. [In Syria and Barbary Hê▵e el is vulgarly shortened into Hel indeclinable; which confounds it with the interrogative particle (Art. 42). For farther emphasis they say Hel rajol hê▵e, this very man.]

33. If This, That, is to be joined to the *second* of two composite nouns, nothing new arises. They say, ᶻIsm hê▵e el xaiᶻ, the name (of) this thing; Sebab hê▵e el xofl, the cause (of) this business, exactly as Awâmir el melic el kaiyir, the commands (of) the benign king. Nay, even if This or That be isolated, we can say, Sebab hê▵e, the cause (of) this; Liᶻejl ▵êlic (on account (of) that.

But if This, That, have to be joined to the *former* noun, it is better to throw the demonstrative to the end, as, This son (of) the king, Ibn el melic hê▵e; where Hêde agrees with Ibn, not with Melic. [In 23 it has been noted that Loqman in a certain phrase violates this rule.]

It is also popular to adopt Turkish idiom so far as to say, "This king, his son," for "The son of this king;" thus leaving *king* without any regimen at all. It is a liberty which adds one more element of vagueness to a syntax already vexatiously vague.

34. We proceed to speak on the substitutes for our COPULA VERB; is, are; is not, are not. It has appeared that *is*, *are*, are very often understood. Yet we cannot say, Hêᴧe el TaTTâr, for, This (is) the druggist; for the words will mean, This druggist. In such cases we must use Hou (he) or Hie (she) for *is*, and Hom, *f*. Honna (they), for *are*. In fact, Hou also stands for *am*, *art*, which strikingly testifies to the loss of its original sense. The learner must habituate himself to these uses of Hou, Hie, Hom, Honna. Houa, Hiya, Homma, are *more emphatic* than Hou, Hie, Hom, and seem to be a modern improvement. (C. de Perceval remarks on Honna as used for the masculine; but this is clearly inadmissible.)

35. Examples:

Hêhona mây Taᴧib, here (is) sweet water.
Hêᴧe el mây hou bârid jiddan, this water is very cold.
Honâ el kobz hou Taiyib, here the bread is good.
Honêc el mây morr, there the water (is) bitter.
Honêlie el kamr leᴧieᴧ, yonder the wine (is) delicious.
Hêᴧe el nebieᴧ Hölou ceθieran, this toddy (is) too sweet.
ᴧêlic Husân jaiyid, yonder one (is) an excellent horse.
ᴧêlic el Husân hou jaiyid, yonder horse is excellent.
Tile el dâr hie Hasena jiddan, yonder house is very handsome.
Tile el kail kafiefe, yonder horses (are) light (swift).
ᴧêlic el bafl el aHmar melieH, yonder red mule (is) good.
Heᴧêc bafl melieH, that (here is) a fine mule.
Hêola hom nês milâH, these are good men.
Collo xai⁼ honâ cowaiyis, everything here is pretty.
Hêᴧe hou miθl heᴧêc, this is like that.
Hêᴧe el semn mâliH ceθieran, this butter is too salt.

N.B.—Melieh in old style is *fair*, καλός : but, like each of those words, has changed its sense to Good in general. East of Syria for Good they seem to prefer Zeiÿin, Zein, which means Adorned, Fine. For Mây (water) at Aleppo they use M'wai, *i.e.* the diminutive Mowaiy. See Art. 84 below.

36. To omit *is* often leaves the syntax obscure : to omit *there is* is worse. For the latter the best direct substitute is, Youjad, literally, it is found (= it exists, it can be had) or the participle Maujoud, found; as, El Tüfr youjad (*or* maujoud) honêe, the (red) stag is found there. For *is* we may sometimes say, Sâr, is become. In classical style, not quite obsolete, we have also the following substitute :

Inni, I am ; Innec (*m.*) thou art; Inneho, he is.
Innena, we are ; Innecom, ye are ; Innehom, they are.
(See 55 below.)
Qolt, *enna* hê△ih el sefara *innehe* menḥouse, I said, *that* this voyage *is verily* unlucky.

[In Barbary the imperative Râ, see ! is used to the same effect : Râni (see me! *i.e.*) I am ; Rêe, thou art ; Rêh, he is, etc. In the Bagdad pashâlic, they say *écou* for There is; which perhaps means Hê-com, "lo for you!" In Aleppo (what is worst of all) they say, Fichi, *in it*, to mean There is, Il *y* a. All these methods, being purely local, are displeasing to the learned, and to all who aspire at a universal Arabic.]

37. "Is not, Are not," are, Leis, *f.* Leiset, *pl.* Leisou. These are classical, and still in use. More popular are : Mâ hou, *f.* Mâ hie, is not; *pl.* Mâ hom, are not. Mâ is the modern particle of *negation*, Lâ generally that of *prohibition ;*

but it is highly inconvenient that Ma is also interrogative and relative. Nevertheless, even in ancient Arabic, Mâ ana hou, means Non ego sum, I am not. [Mâ hou is contracted to *M'ou* in Syria; and Mâ hou xai⁵ (is not a thing, *i.e.* is not a whit, is not at all) into *M'oux'*.]

38. Hêᴀih el medicna leiset qadiema jiddan, this city is not very ancient.

Honâ mâ* youjad kobz ⁷ari, here is not found fresh bread.

Hêola el nês leisou mok⁷urien, these men are not dangerous (*pl.*).

Leis hêhona ka⁷ar qa⁷, there is not here danger at all.

Mâ hou xai⁵ honêc, there is nothing there.

Kobz ⁷ari leis mo⁵uḤḤ, fresh bread is not wholesome.

Hou fair mo⁵uḤḤ, is unwholesome.

The predicate in classical style has a strange tendency to take the preposition Bi (in, with) after it; as, Leis bi kâyin, he is not a traitor. This redundant *bi* is neither necessary nor popular.

39. The emphatic pronouns of 1st and 2nd person are:

Ana, I.	Ent, thou (*m.* Entè, *f.* Enti).
Naḥn, Naḥna, we (Barb. Aḥna).	Entom, ye (*f.* Entonna).

And a classical dual, Entomâ, ye two.

Classical and also current are:

Lest, I am not.	Lesna, we are not.
Lest, *f.* Lesti, thou art not.	Lestom, ye are not.

---

* Unless we discriminate *mâ* from *mă*, this sentence may mean: "Here *what* is found *is* fresh bread."

40. Examples:

Ana bardân* jiddan,
    I (am) very cold.
Ṭase ente jauṭân,
    perhaps thou (art) hungry.
Ana lest ṬaṬxân,
    I am not thirsty.
Ente ᴀou ṭaql,
    thou art intelligent.
Lesna ᴀewic' mâl,
    we are not wealthy.
Ana hou el melic,
    I am the king.
Lest ana kâdim,
    I am not a servant.
Ente hou el moṭallim,
    thou art the teacher.

Naḥna hom foqarâ,
    we are poor.
Lestom afniyâ,
    ye are not rich.
Mâ ana hou ᴀou mâl,
    I am not wealthy.
Robbama ente kâyif,
    possibly thou (art) afraid.
Ana mâ kâyif qaṬ,
    I am not afraid at all.
Ente jesour ceθieran,
    thou art too daring.
Ṭase entè ṭair jesour,
    perhaps thou art not daring.

41. The word *such* is associated by us with the demonstratives; so also is *same*. *Such* is compounded of so-like in English (solche, swilke, swa-leiks), and the Arabs also express it thus at large by miθl hêᴀe, or, miθlihêᴀe, which virtually becomes a single word, and might be so written. If a noun follows, El must come between, as Miθlihêᴀe el rajol, such *a* man. How *same* is to be expressed will presently appear.

---

* A person who *feels* cold or warm is bardân, dafyân; but a thing that *imparts* cold or warmth is bârid, dâfi; as, mây bârid, cold water; ridâ dâfi, a warm mantle.

§ 4. INTERROGATIVES.

42. The Interrogative *Particles* may first be attended to. In English we put the nominative after the verb (as, Is it? Has he?) and thus dispense with a particle. The Latins use An, -ne, Utrum, Num; and especially in writing, these are needed for perspicuity. In Arab talk, the tone of voice suffices to denote that a question is asked; yet Faris and Kayat (two extremes) agree in exhibiting the interrogative particles E? Hel? in a context emphatically modern. Thus:

Hou faṣuiḤ,	Hêᴧe leis ṣaḤuiḤ,
he is eloquent.	this is not true.
E hou faṣuiḤ?	E fa leis hêᴧe ṣaḤuiḤ?
is he eloquent?	is not then this true?
Hel ente el ṬaṬṬâr?	Hel el ṣabi ṭafi?
art thou the druggist?	is the boy hale and well?

43. If an alternative is put (as in Latin *Utrum-an*) the word Or, which introduces the second member, is expressed by Em; as:

E hou akƛar? *em* ezraq?
is it green? *or* blue?

The particle Fa (then) often follows the interrogative E; thus with negatives we have E-lâ—? E-fa-lâ—? E-mâ—? E-fa-leis—? is it not? is it not then? But for the *past* time Lem replaces Lâ; as Au-e-lem—? or *was* it not?

44. Interrogative *Substantive* Mán, who? Má? Mâᴧe? what? *Adjective: m.* Ei, Eiyo; *f.* Ei, Eiya; which? what? as: Ei rajol, what man? which man? Eiya marˤa, what woman?

Adverbs: Ein, where? | Cém, how much? how many?
Ila‛ein, whither? | Ceif, how?
Min‛ein, whence? | Em'te, when?

45. Em'te is compounded of E mete. The classical Mete is either interrogative or relative. In modern use Mete is relative, and even so, it is rarer than Lemma, when; and Em'te expresses "when?" interrogatively.

Ei (what? which?) is of both numbers as well as genders. In Syria they use Eina, like *quisnam*. Mâ∆e, what? well supersedes Má, which has too many senses. Vulgarly also *Eix'* (*i.e.* Ei xai‛, what thing?) is prevalent; but this ought not to be followed by a noun, since it has the noun xai‛ within it.

46. *Man*, following a noun, may mean " of whom;" as, Beit mán hê∆e? house (of) whom (is) this? but it is surely better to say, Li mán hê∆e el bait? to whom (belongs) this house?

Manou? Man hou? are often heard, especially when the word stands alone: indeed classically, Manou? is nominative, and Manâ? accusative. The latter is obsolete.

Má, adverbially, may qualify an adjective, with the sense How! in admiration: as, Má ana mescien! how wretched I (am)!

47. The words Man, Ma, Cem, admit of becoming "indefinite" instead of interrogative; *i.e.* mean *some, any, a certain quantity*. To suggest the right sense, I find it useful to copy Greek accentuation; and write Mán, Má, Cém, when they are interrogative; and Màn, Mà, Cèm, when they are indefinite. In fact, it is natural to elevate the musical tone when words are interrogative.

Man, Ma, Ei, Ein, Ceif, admit also of becoming *Relatives*, as will afterwards be noted.

48. Mân hou honêc? who is there?
    Ei Ḥaiwân hou hêᴀe? what animal is this?
    Ei marᶜa? Eina marᶜa? Eiyat imrâᶜa? what woman?
    E lâ eᶜḤad honâ? is not any one here?
    Ei hou (Eina hou) el baſl el qawi? which is the strong mule?
    Ein el ʿsabi el ʿsaſier? where is the little boy?
    Hel youjad laḤm honêlic? is meat (to be) found yonder?
    E fa lâ ente bardân? art not thou then cold?
    Eiyat hie el Ḥör'mat el moḤsine? which is the beneficent lady?

§ 5. PREPOSITIONS.

49. The primary prepositions should all be learned at once. They are:

Bi, in, with, by.	Maʿï (together), with.
Ce, according to, like.	ʿFala', upon, against.
Fie, in, into.	ʿFand, with, at, long.
Ila', to (with motion).	(French *chez*, apud.)
Li, to, for.	ʿFan, off from, away from,
Min, from, of.	concerning.

Of these, Ce is the least popular. It is superseded by Miθl, like. It enters into Ceᴀê, like this, so; Hêceᴀê, thus, so (vulg. Heic); Ceᴀêlic, like that, so forth, likewise: and in Syria (from the classical Ce-ma, *selon que*, according as) has come Cemân, "likewise, again." It is right also to say, Ce miθl, *ad instar*, after the fashion of. Ceʌê is used for *such*, as, Li ceʌê rajol, to such a man. See Art. 41, above. The article El coalesces with some of the above, making Bil, Cel, Fil, Ila'l, Lil, Ƭala'l. [The vulgar say Fiel, but Fil is classical.] Ila' and Ƭala' have lost *y* which they sometimes resume.

50. Of the other prepositions, some are of less immediate importance to the learner, yet it may be convenient to have a list here.

About (of quantity), naƕou.
Above, fauq, feuq.
According to, tebaƮ.
After (of time), baƮd.
Against, Ďudd.
Agreeably to, Ƭubq.
Among, min jomlet; bain.
Around, ƕaul.
Before, qabl.
Behind, warâ, kalf.
Below, Beneath, Under, teƕt.
Beside (at side of), ladâ, ladon, janb.
Besides, mă Ƭadâ.
Between, bain, fie mă bain.
Concerning, min naƕou.
Contrary to, kilâf.
During, dawâm, Ƭöul.

Except, ƒair, kalâ, Ƭadâ, sewâ.
In exchange for, bidâl.
In front of, qoddâm, qobâla(t).
In presence of, ˁemâm.
In proportion to, ƕaseb.
Instead of, mecên, Ƭawaď, Ƭuwaďan Ƭan.
Like, miθl, ce miθl.
Opposite, tojàh, tilqâ.
Over against (face to face with—*vis-à-vis*) ƕudê, izê.
Provided not, ƕaxâ.
Since (of time), monʌ, moʌʌ.
Together with, Ʒoƕbat.
Towards, naƕou.
Until, Till, ƕatte', li ƕadd.

Within, dâkil; *vulg.* jou-wa(t).
Without, ⎫ kârij,
Outside of, ⎭ *vulg.* barra(t).

Without (Lat. *sine*), bilâ, bi ſair, min ſair, ſair; bi doun, min doun.

51. Miθli (for Ce-miθli, after the likeness) is very popular in place of Ce. For *like* are also said Naʒuir, Xibh. Ĩair, before an adjective, was explained *Not;* its sense *Without* displays analogy to German and Greek in forming a negative adjective from Ohne, ἄνευ, without. But Ĩair means *difference, diverse from.* Naḧöu, towards, about, is used to modify a substantive, as the Latins use *quasi,* "as it were;" in popular English, "a sort of." Thus, ḧaul el wejh naḧöu cenâr eswad, around the face (is), *as it were,* a black border— *a sort of* black border. A preposition will then, if needed by the noun, precede Naḧöu. Thus, Fie naḧöu ʒörra, in *a sort of* bundle. The word Naḧöu simply adds vagueness, and may influence several nouns coupled by Wa, and. Ϸöul el joθθa naḧöu θelêθ aqdâm, the length of the body is *about* three feet; but it may equally be rendered, "is *towards* three feet." Thus the word vacillates between preposition and adverb.

In some connections Ϸan seems to mean *without*: thus, Entè ſani ʔannoh; Enti ſanieya ʔannoh, thou art rich without it, *i.e.* thou canst dispense with it.

Ma-ʔada and Sewâ have the vexatious ambiguity of *Præter* and Beside(s), meaning either "except" or "in addition to." Sewâ as a popular adverb means, "side by side, abreast." Ma-ʔada strictly means "what passes."

Lada, Ladon, may be called high style. They are used

especially (like old Greek παρὰ) in such connections as, At the side of the king; so, Min lada el melic, from the side of the king.

52. Uses of *Min*. In locomotion it is contrasted to Ila; as, "*from* Rome *to* London;" which needs no farther remark: its use for "of," is less regular. The deficiency of "of" in Arabic is supplied, partly by composition of nouns, partly by Min and Li, partly by special evasion or provincial methods. Min differs from Ƭan nearly as Latin *ab* or *ex* from *de*. Ƭan, like *de*, may mean "concerning." Min expresses the partitive idea of *ex;* also the material of a thing. It likewise enables us to put El (the) to either of two related nouns. Examples:

 LauƜ min Ɯajar, a slab of stone.
 Bâb min kaxab, a door of timber.
 Ceθier min el marâcib, many of the ships.
 Cém min el marâcib? how many of the ships?
 SebƬa min el Yahoud, seven of the Jews.
 QaƮuiƮ min el maƭz, a flock of goats.
 El marꞃa' min el foqarâ, the sick (ones of the) poor.
 Elf Ʈabaq min el waraq, a thousand layers of paper.
 Miqdâr wâfir min ᶜewâni, a copious quantity of vessels.
 JamâƬa Ƭaʒuima min el nês, a vast company of men.
 El himma min el chêli, the earnestness of the population.
 Mablaſ min el noqoud, an amount (sum) of cash.
 Cém min el mosêfirien? how many of the travellers?
 El kobz râdi, melꞌên min el raml, the bread (is) bad (and) full of sand.
 Kams firaq min el jonoud, five companies of troops.

Hêᴀe hou wahmieya min el Ꭻabaꞇuiya, this is a fantasy of the police.

El foꞃöun el ꞇawiele min el xajara, the long boughs of the tree.

Wâbil min el Ꭻarb, a shower of beating.

El qaḢꞇ min el akbâr, the dearth of news.

El sêꞇat el θêniya min el ꞃabâḤ, the second hour of the morning.

El ꞇaraf el ximâli min el jeziera, the north side of the island.

Firꞇ min silc el telefrâf, a branch of the wire (of) the telegraph.

Wezier min daulat Americce, a minister of the government (of) America.

Jonaineti min ward, my garden of roses.

53. For, What sort of?—they say, Eix' min—? as, Eix' min ꞇair? what sort of bird? (Comp. Germ. *Was für ein*—.)

With the partitive Of, the Arabs often repeat a noun, instead of using Eʻḣad (one) pronominally; thus, for One *of* the king's cities, they say, not only, Uḣda' min modon el melic, but also, Mediena min modon el melic; and stiff as the latter appears, it is popular, as well as classical. So for Fie ᴀêt leil, on a certain night, they also say, In a night of the nights, fie leila min el leyêli. *Min* is also used like French *du, dela*, to mean Some, A portion of; as, Min soccer, some sugar; especially in repetition, Minhom—minhom, some of them—and others of them.

54. In ambitious prose, Min is used to satiety in the predicate of a proposition, to make it indefinite. Thus instead

of Hêᴀe mosteḣuil, this is absurd; they say, Hêᴀe min el mosteḣuil, c'(est) (une chose) d'absurde. Thus we are more than ever kept in suspense where the predicate will be found. The formula *Minma*, from what, *i.e.* "from that which," is similarly abused: as, Hêᴀe minma yoḣayyir el bâl, this (is) (a thing) of the things which perplex the mind; where, if *minna* were simply left out, the sense would be correct enough and the grammar perfect. When a copula-verb (as Cên, was) is expressed, all is clear, though Eʿḣad (one) be omitted before Min: as, Cên min el ʿomarâ, he was (one) of the princes, erat e principibus.

Min (like our *from*) often means "because of." Likewise, after a passive verb, it takes the sense of our *by*.

55. Uses of *Li*. In general Li, meaning *to* or *for*, needs no further particular remark. But, like the Latin dative, it may be used in the predicate, where popular English uses the nominative. Thus: "It is a marvel to me," may become, "It is to me *for* a marvel." The Arabs even say, Ente innec li jâhil, thou verily art *for* a fool, *i.e.* thou art foolish. Hêᴀe ʿandi li moʿjize, this (is) with me *for* a miracle.

Again, as in Latin, either dative or genitive with Est (is) denotes *possession*, so Li (to) may supply this sense; especially if of two related nouns the governing is indefinite and the governed definite; as, *A* top of *the* mountain, *A* son of *the* king; we may then use Li for English Of, saying Râʿs lil jebal, Ibn lil melic.

Li (for) means also *on account of;* especially with pronouns. Thus, Lihêᴀe, on this account; Liᴀélic, on that account; Li mâᴀe? wherefore? L'eix'? why? (=Li ei xaiʿ?) But with nouns we have generally a paraphrase, as in English.

Liʿejl, Min ejl, for the sake of.
Li sebab, ⎫
Bi sebab, ⎬ because of.
Min jara', in consequence of.

Li xân (Min xân, *vulg.* Alep.), on account of; from Xân, state.

56. Uses of *Bi*. It especially expresses the instrument, or mode, or price; as, To buy a thing, "bi θeman qaliel," *at* or *for* a scanty price; to slay a man, "biḷ seif," *with* or *by* the sword. As expressing the mode, it forms a paraphrase for adverbs and prepositions. Thus:

    Biḷ collieya, in entirety, *i.e.* entirely.
    Biḷ ziyâda, in surplus, superfluously.
    Biḷ fâya, in the extreme, extremely.
    Biḷ raſm ʿan, in spite of.
    Bi moujib, in virtue of.
    Bi wâsiʿat, by means of.
    Bi xiddat, by dint of.
    Bi fair, Bi doun, without.

With verbs of motion, Bi must be rendered *with*, though it still is not identical with Maʿ (together with); but "come *with*" a thing, is said for "bring" it: "to go off with" it, is to carry it off. Many other verbs take Bi after them, just as in Latin and Greek many verbs govern a particular case, for which no reason appears. The idiomatic uses of Bi are very numerous, and are a main difficulty.

§ 6. SUFFIX PRONOUNS.

57. The personal pronouns, attached to prepositions or to nouns, take abridged forms in which the originals are quite disguised.

-ie, -i, -ya, me, my.	m. -ec, -e, f. -ie, -ei, thee, thy.	-ho ? -oh, -hi, him, his.	-hê, her.
-na, us, our.	m. -com, f. -con, you, your.	m. hom ; f. hon, them, their.	

N.B.—After a *verb*, "me" is expressed by -ni. The rest are the same after a verb as after a preposition.

In the spoken language, -com and -hom are freely used of both genders, and the duals -comâ (you two), -homâ (them two), are not heard. To express "*it*," the feminine -hê is often used. It is inconvenient, that, in speaking of *things*, hê in classical style constantly means *them*.

The suffix, like a Greek enclitic, often changes the accent of the preceding word, and sometimes hereby lengthens a vowel; thus, Mélice, queen, Meliécti, my queen. At other times it cuts out a vowel; as, SélTana, empire; SelTán'ti, my empire.

Thee, Thy, after a long vowel, is -e for the masculine, -ei for the feminine. [But at Bagdad it is always -ei; in Algiers, it seems, m. and f. are the same.]

58. System to exhibit all the forms.

Bie, Biya	Lie, Liya	Ileiya	Minni
Bee	Lee	Ileie	Minnee, Mine
Biei (f.)	Liei	Ileiei	Minnie (*Alep.*)
Bihi, Boh	Liho, Loh	Ileihi	Minnoh, Minho
Bihê	Lihê,	Ileihê	Minhê
Bina	etc.	Ileina,	Minna
Bicom, -n.		etc.	Mincom,
Bihom, -n.			etc.

Ṭandi	Baini	Qábli	Citêbi
Ṭandac	Bainec	Qablac	Citêbec
Ṭaudic	Bainic	Qablic	Citêbic
Ṭandoh	Bainoh	Qabloh	Citêboh
Ṭandahê	Bainahe	Qáblahe	Cithêbahê
Ṭandana,	Bainana,	Qablana,	Citêbana
etc.	etc.	etc.	etc.

59. Him, his, is ordinarily pronounced -ô, as in Hebrew, no *h* being heard; but after a long vowel, all authorities bid us pronounce only -*h*. An Englishman who tries to sound -*h*, is apt to turn it into E. I think by pronouncing -*hi* with as short an *i* as he can manage, he will come nearest to the sound; and *hi*, after all, is classical. [Classical rules bid us say -*hi*, -*him*, -*hinna*, -*hima*, when a vowel of the *i* class precedes. The learner may at his pleasure so modify the *o* of these words. I observe that Faris, as also Léon and Hélot in Loqman's Fables, equally with Catafago, give Fie waqt*oh*, Ila dâr*oh*, etc., and do not struggle for Fie waqt*ihi*, Ila dâr*ihi*, etc. Cherbonneau vacillates.]

60. Examples:

Ommi marieẊa jiddan, my mother is very ill.
Aboui (Abi) wa ommi marẊa', my father and my mother are ill.
Hel abouc Ṭaiyib? is thy father alive and well?
Zeujati hie Ṭaiyiba, my wife is alive and well.
Ommec Ṭase Ṭaiyiba? thy mother perhaps is alive and well?
Ceif Ḥâlec? how is thy state (thy health)?
Eix' bec? Mâᴧe bec? what ails thee?
Leis xai⁺ biya, nothing ails me.
Hel hêᴧe lec? is this thine?

Mâ hou liya, it is not mine.
Hêt ma Ṭandec! bring what thou hast.
Leis Ṭandi xai', I have nothing.
Mâᴀe fie bâlec? what is in thy mind?
Mâ hou xai⁵ fie bâli, there is nothing in my mind.
Ṭalaiya Ṭaila, on me (rests) a family.
Liho aulâd Ṣugâr, he has little children.
Lec baqara melieḥa, thou hast a fine cow.
Lihê qoroun Ṭawiele, she has long horns.
Ommi hie maṬ oktec, my mother is with thy sister.
Héhona hie ommec, here is thy mother.
Ein aboui (abi) el⁵ên?* where (is) my father now?
Abouc fil belda, thy father (is) in town.
Akouc leis fie bilâdina, thy brother is not in our country.
Ṭandana abouc héhona, thy father is with us here.
Ṭalaiya morâdec el Ṭaziez, on me (rests) thy esteemed wish
    (*i.e.* I will try to perform it).
Akouh rajol melieḥ, his brother is a good man.
Collohom nês milâḥ, all of them are good men.
Collocom ᴀewie' himma, all of you are endowed with earnest-
    ness, *i.e.* are earnest, energetic.
Hel okti Ṭandacom el⁵ên? is my sister with you now?
Honâ âki maṬ oktec, here is my brother with your sister.
Leis maṬui kobz Ṭari, I have no fresh bread with me.
MaṬac Ṭase† folous, you have perhaps small cash with you.

---

* Father, Brother, have radicals ʿbw, ʿkw, yet are absolutely expressed by Ab, Ak, but in composition the *w* reappears regularly in popular style; as, Aboui, my father; Akoui, my brother; though Aki is also heard. Aboui is not classical, though Abou followed by a noun is.

† Ṭase, *perhaps*, is said of hope or fear; and serves to ask a question.

Eiyoma ꞇandec, hêtoh ileiya, whatever thou hast, bring it to me.

Colloma maꞇac, hêtoh ila honâ, all that is with you, bring it hither.

△êlic el Ḧuṡân, e lâ houa lec? yonder horse, is he not thine?

Mán hou maꞇac fiḷ dâr? who is with thee in the house?

Mâ ꞇandi cotob, I have no books.

Leiset ꞇandana aqlâm, we have no pens.

Cên liya ꞌâk, I had a brother.

The particle Ce is never prefixed to a suffix pronoun. We must enlarge it into Ce-miθli or Miθli: thus, He is not like me, Mâ hou miθliey(a); He is like you, Houa miθlec (or miθlic).

61. ꞇan, like Min, popularly doubles its *n* before some of the suffixes. Li, according to classical rule, becomes Le or La with suffixes. The sole trace of this seems to be in Loh or Leho (never Lih*i*) for *to him* (Le means *verily*). Catafago writes Lici, Lihê, Lina, Lihom. C. de Perceval and De Braine are silent as to L*a*ho, L*a*na, etc., which my ear certainly never caught. Lie, Lec, are to be divided L-ie, L-ec (sounded as English *lack*). Liya, Biya are perhaps more emphatic than Lie, Bie. In Aleppo Boh prevails over Bihi, yet Bihi is thought better. Cherbonneau writes B'ho even in poetry.

62. ꞇand is written with *kisra* (*i.e.* as ꞇund) by modern literati; yet C. de Perceval, in doing this, defines the sound by French *dnd*. I never heard in this word any vowel but a clear French *a*. Dictionaries exhibit ꞇand, ꞇund, ꞇönd as on a par; hence we have no motive to struggle against the popular practice.

63. Several particles assume pronouns suffix. Inna (verily) was named above; Enna (that) does the same; also Lecinna, nevertheless: thus, Lecinni, yet I; Lecinnec, yet thou; Lecinnoh, yet he; Lecinnena, yet we, etc. The vowel of union which appears in Ƭand*a*he, Bain*a*na, Citêb*a*na, etc., must be looked on, in the present stage of the language, as purely euphonic. All prepositions ending in two consonants are apt to need this vowel of union. The learner must not be seduced by the aspect of Qabl-na to pronounce it Qabalna.

64. Lehê Ƭainain* jamieletein, she has beautiful eyes.

Leho zeuja jamiele, he has a beautiful wife.

Ƭandoh ᶜehl eeθier, *chez lui* is a numerous household.

Leho Ƭaila wâfira, he has an abundant (numerous) family.

Aulâdec maƬui fil rief, thy children are with me in the country (*ruri*).

Hêᴀe hou Ƭalaihi, this is his duty.

Mâᴀe liya Ƭalaie (Ƭandee)? what art thou to pay me?

Qadd eix' bi weddee? how much dost thou want?

Leis xaiᶻ Ƭalaiya lee, I owe thee nothing.

Leis xaiᶻ liya, illa farxain, I have nothing, but two piastres.

Dâree fasieĥa, zeiyine, thy house is spacious (and) fine.

Dâri miθli dâree, my house is like thine.

Cilâhomâ† sewâ sewâ, both of the two are on a par.

65. As the examples just given may suggest, Ƭand, Li, MaƬ, Ƭala are in great use, to supply the verbs Have, Owe, Ought Ƭandi, I have in my house, or in my possession; Liya, I have in ownership; MaƬui, I have with me, about

---

* More classical Ƭainân—tên.
† Perhaps Cilâhoma is too high style. Cilâ(n), *both*, is dual; oblique case, Cileï'. It is too good a word to lose.

me. Thus, Maîac siccieneti? (have you) my knife with you? Ṭandi Ḧuṣân, mâ hou liya, I have a horse, (but) he does not belong to me.

Debt or Duty is said to rest *upon* or *against* the debtor: hence Ṭalaiya, I owe; Ṭalaiya folous lec, I owe thee small cash.

66. The suffix (possessive) must be repeated with each noun which we desire it to affect. Thus, "His will and pleasure," becomes, "His will and *his* pleasure," Irâdetoh wa kâṭuroh.

67. For emphasis they say, Liya ana, to me myself; Minnec ente, from thee thyself, etc. Also Eiyâ, as a fulcrum, enables a pronoun in the oblique case to be isolated: thus, Ʒanant-ec eiyâc, "I thought thee (to be) thyself." Eiyâc naṭbod, wa eiyâc nesteṭuin, "thee we adore, and thee we call to aid." When a verb takes two pronouns after it, one of them must be thus isolated in the modern dialect.

68. If a demonstrative and a suffix belong to one noun, the demonstrative must follow: as Baſli hêᴧe, this my mule. Similarly with an adjective, as, Baſli el melieḦ, my excellent mule. N.B.—The suffix is understood to make the noun *definite*.

§ 7. AUXILIARY NOUNS, OR QUASI-PRONOUNS.

69. In English the nouns Self, Sake, Behalf, and others, have lost much of their substantive nature: Self, in particular, has almost degenerated into a pronoun. The same is the case with many Arab nouns. Peculiarly, Nefs (soul), *pl.* Nofous or generally Anfos, does duty for Self; as do ᴧêt,

essence, personality; Ḣâl, state; Rouḣ, spirit, *pl.* Arwâḣ; and even Ϯain, eye. We may add Mâl, property; Ḣaqq, right; which, though abused provincially, seem to have a legitimate use in harmony with good grammar. △êt, *pl.* △ewât, has too many senses. Besides being an adjective pronoun, as explained in Art. 31 (as, Ḣoqoul △êt Ḣösn, fields *endowed with* beauty), and (what is perhaps quite old fashioned) Fie △êt yeum, on a *certain* day; it is also much used politically, as, El̦ △êt el̦ sol Ϯânieya, the imperial self (person); El̦ △ewât el cirâm, the noble personages. Catafago says absolutely, △êt, a lady.

70. Examples:

Ṣabi rama' nefsoh fil̦ nehr, a boy threw *himself* into the river.
El Ϯarab enfóshom, the Arabs themselves.
Arouḣ ana bi △êti, I will go in my person (myself).
Qatel Ḣâl-oh, *or* rouḣi-oh, he slew himself.
Qâl fie nefsoh, *or* li Ḣâloh, he said in his soul (to himself).
Yaxcor rouḣoh, Yamdaḣ nefsoh, he thanks (he praises) himself.
El Ḣuṣân mâloh, the horse his property, *i.e.* his *own* horse.
El Ḣaql Ḣaqqi, the field my right, *i.e.* my *own* field.
El emier Ϯainoh, the prince himself.

But Ϯain peculiarly is used to supply the word *Same;* as, Fil yeum Ϯainoh, (*or* Ϯainihi), in that day itself, in that same day. Meteϯ, a piece of property (an article, as we say), *pl.* Emtiϯa, is said to serve, especially in Africa, as Mâl, to express what is one's own. Mâl, Meteϯ, and Ḣaqq may sometimes conduce to emphasis and clearness, in connections where at first sight they are vulgar superfluity. Thus, El̦ darâhim,

Ḥaqq el jouk, means, "the money *due* for the woollen cloth," literally, "the money, the right of the cloth."

71. But at Moosul or Bagdad I wrote down from the mouths of the people the following redundancies; suggesting that Mâl has become a mere preposition, Of.

Dibs mâl Ḥaleb,	Laḥm mâl kinzier,
treacle of Aleppo.	meat of hog.
Dibs mâl zebieb,	El Ṣandouq mâl el jemal,
treacle of raisins.	the box of the camel.
Zebieb mâl dibs,	El Ḥalieb mâl el ṣöbḥ,
raisins of treacle.	the milk of the morning, *i.e.* fresh.

No such phraseology would be admitted in literature. Whether Mâli, Mâlec, ... in the predicate for Mine, Thine, ... would pass, is also questionable. At Bagdad instead of the classical "Hêᴅi citêbi wa heᴅêc citêbec," this is my book, and this is *thy book* (which seems to an Englishman so very flat), they say, Hêᴅe citêbi wa heᴅêc *mâlec*. Though Mine, Thine .... are expressible simply by Liya, Lec .... (as, Mâ hou liya, it is not mine) nevertheless, Hêᴅe citêbi wa heᴅêc lec, would be wanting in contrast and point.

72. It may seem that they can evade the double genitive (24) by Mâl or Metêṭ; as, Celb, metêṭ el melic, *a* hound, *the* property of the king. Both C. de Perceval and de Braine lay down that in such connection the former noun *must* be preceded by El; which of course is the case when nothing is meant but "*the* hound of the king." But perhaps in the opposite case they would prefix Wâḥud to Celb, for fear of being thought to omit El by accident.

73. We might enumerate as auxiliary *adjectives* or participles, not only E⁵Ḥad, Wâḥud, but also Makʃöuʃ (belonging, *peculiar*, proper), Meᴀcour (afore-named). Thus, Ibni el makʃöuʃ, my proper son, my own son; El ʃabi el meᴀcour, the aforesaid boy. Indeed Meᴀcour seems to have none of the stiffness which we feel in *aforesaid, aforenamed*, but has wide currency. Like to it are the formulas, El moxâr ileihi, the alluded-to; El mouma' ileihi, the hinted-at, the pointed-at.

74. Ṭadda, a number; Jomla, a group; are used like the English *several*, to express an indefinite number. A short list of the indefinite words often called pronominal may here be convenient.

All, coll, jamieʔ.
Each, coll wâḥud.
A certain, wâḥud (before its noun).
Any one (*quispiam, quisquam*, after If or a negative), e⁵ḥad, *f.* uḥda'.
Any (positively), eiyoman cên, *quivis*, ciyoma cên, *quodvis*.
None, lâ e⁵ḥad.
Not even one, wala wâḥud.
Several, Ṭuddat, jomlat (*a number*).
Both (*ambo*), cilci (classical nom. cilê).
Some, baʔʃ (i.e. *a part*).

One—another; baʔʃ—baʔʃ; màn—màn.
Some—others; baʔʃ—baʔʃ; minhom—minhom; minhe—minhe.
Some (ones), *aliquot;* cèm wâḥud.
Other, e⁵kar, *f.* ⁵okra', *pl.* ⁵ekâra, ⁵ekarien.
Other (diverse), ſair—before noun.
The Rest, el sê⁵ir.
Several, } xette'.
Divers, }
Some or other, mà (after noun).

"Others than he," in classical style, is variously rendered by Ma ϯadàhi (what passes him), Ma sewâhi (what is on his level), and Γairoh, his diverse (?). The roots of ϯadâ and Sewâ mean Inequality and Equality.

BaϯΛ (not repeated) is also now used for *one another*; but it seems, incorrectly.

It was stated (47) that Man, Ma, may become indefinite; hence the Màn—màn; and Rejâ mà, *some* hope *or other*. The latter phrase is found in modern literature, and is classical. Freitag renders it *qualiscunque*.

75. Γair is regarded as a substantive by grammarians. Hence with a suffix, Γairhom, others than they; Γairoh, other than he; and even absolutely, El Γair, some one else, thy diverse(?), thy neighbour, in ethical relation. Sewâ, Sowa', *even, like;* is ridiculously explained in lexicons to mean, 1. The same; 2. The opposite; [égal; même chose; autre.] Γair xai⁵, *quite* another thing, a different thing, is stronger than Xai⁵ eʿkar, another thing, a second thing. So with the negative, Leis ce miθliho fie Γair mecên, in *no other* place is anything like it. At the close of a sentence, Là Γair, lâ Γairoh, nothing else, is used dogmatically, for "so, and so only."

§ 8. NUMERALS.

76. Wâḧud, *f.* Wâḧuda, means *one, a single one, alone.* So we have, Waḧidi, I alone; Waḧdee, thou alone; Waḧdoh, he alone; Waḧdana, we alone, etc., with all the suffix pronouns. Let us here repeat: Wâḧud, one (emphatical), follows its noun; as, Fie ḧaql wâḧud, in one field. But,

Fie wâḥud ḥaql, means,—in a certain field. But besides; Eʿḥad, *f.* Uḥda', is *one* in a pronominal use; which may also be rendered *any one* (quisquam, quispiam); as, Lâ eʿḥad, not any; but Wâḥud, some one (aliquis, quidam); Wala wâḥud, not even one (ne unus quidem).

77. The numerals from 3 to 10 collectively take plural nouns, and have the peculiarity that the feminine form looks like masculine and the masculine like feminine. The numerals from 11 to 19 are contracted in modern speech, and have a still shorter vulgar form, which is probably destined to become standard. *Six* is anomalous; analogy requires Sidse.

1 wâḥud, *f.* wâḥuda.	11 uḥdaʿxar (ḥudaʿx).
2 iθnein, *f.* iθnetein.	12 iθnaʿx(ar).
3 θelêθe, *f.* θelêθ.	13 θelêθetaʿx(ar).
4 arbaʿa, *f.* arbaʿ.	14 arbaʿtaʿx(ar).
5 kamse, *f.* kams.	15 kams'taʿx(ar).
6 sitte, *f.* sitt.	16 sittetaʿxar (sittâʿx).
7 sebʿa, *f.* sebʿ.	17 sebʿataʿx(ar).
8 θemânia, *f.* θemân.	18 θemâniataʿxar (θemantaʿx).
9 tisʿa, *f.* tisʿ.	
10 ʿaxara, *f.* ʿaxar.	19 tisʿataʿx(ar).

½ nuʿf.	⅙ sods, *pl.* esdâs.
⅓ θolθ.	⅐ sobʿ, *pl.* esbâʿ.
⅔ θolθein.	⅛ θomn, *pl.* eθmân.
¼ robʿ, *pl.* arbâʿ.	⅑ tosʿ, *pl.* etseʿ.
⅕ koms, *pl.* akmâs.	1/10 ʿoxr, *pl.* aʿxâr.

The final -a, -e, of the masculines from 3 to 10, becomes -at, -et, at least before a vowel; yet I used to hear (I believe), Sitte rijâl, six men; Sittet ʿomara, six princes.

78. For the sake of classifying the imperfect plurals of the language, the following table may deserve to be committed to memory.

                                                                      TYPES.

3 suns, θelêθ xomous (solar plural). . . . . Doroub.
4 moons, arbaʿat aqmâr (lunar plural) . . . Eswâr.
5 men, kamse(t) rijâl (manly plural) . . . . Cilâb.
6 princes, sittet ʿomarâ (princely plural) . . . Wozerâ.
7 merchants, sebʿa(t) tojjâr (mercantile plural). Cottêb.
8 horses, θemâniat aḣʿuna (dactylic plural). . Emcina.
9 { grooms, tisʿa(t) golmân } (false dual) . . { Boldân.
  { legs, tisʿ sieqân   }   { Nierân.
10 cities, ʿaxar modon (short plural) . . . . Borec.

Contrary to analogy, the gender of the *singular* noun is remembered in adapting the numeral to its plural.

79. The remaining cardinals are understood from:

20 ʿuxrién.	21 wâḣud wa ʿuxrien.
30 θelêθién.	32 iθnein wa θelêθien.
40 arbaʿúin.	43 θelêθe wa arbaʿuin.
50 kamsién.	121 mieya wa wâḣud wa ʿuxrien.
60 sittién.	357 θelêθ mieya wa sebʿa wa kamsien.
70 sebʿúin.	7465 sebʿ elâf wa arbaʿ mieya wa
80 θemânién.	kamse wa sittien.
90 tisʿúin.	The units always precede the tens,
100 mieya.	and *mieya* remains singular, against the
1000 ʿclf, *pl.* êlêf.	general rule.

The cardinal numeral when undefined generally precedes its noun, except wâĥud: but El miŧd el arbaʔ, the four stomachs (Faris). "Thousands," in the plural, is also expressible by ʕOlouf; but in numeral composition only Eᶻlêf is employed.

80. The ordinals follow. Auwal (first) has *fem.* Oula'; the other feminines are regular.

2nd θéni(y).	5th kâmis.	8th θêmin.
3rd θêliθ.	6th sêdis.	9th têsiʔ.
4th râbiʔ.	7th sébiʔ.	10th ʔâxir.

Side by side should stand the days of the week.

Sunday,	yeum el eʕĥad.	Thursday, yeum el *kamies*.
Monday,	—— el iθnein.	Friday, —— el jomʔa.
Tuesday,	—— el θelêθe.	Saturday, —— el̩ sebet
Wednesday,	—— el arbaʔa.	(*sabbath*).

81. The ordinals from 20th to 90th (by tens) are the *same* as cardinals; so of 100th, 1000th. In composition, *first* is rendered by Ĥâdi; thus, 21st, Ĥâdi wa ʔuxrien; also 11th, Ĥâdi ʔaxar. So from 11th to 19th ʔaxar is added; as 12th, *m.* θéni ʔaxar, *f.* θéniyat ʔaxara (N.B. with double *fem.* inflexion). And a single article suffices, as El θéni ʔaxar, from 11th to 19th. But above 20th two articles are used, as, *El* Ĥâdi wa *el* ʔuxrien, the 21st (C. de Perceval). [But the old fashioned termination *-oun* supersedes *-ien* in titles.]

For ordinals the order rises from the lower to the higher, units, tens, hundreds, etc.

82. The following is from Caussin de Perceval:—"See here the order in which numbers above a thousand are ex-

pressed. Let us take 3452 : Θelêθet e'lêf wa arbaᵀ mieya, wa iθnein wa khamsien. In this the *tens* are preceded by the units. Dates of *years* are expressed, as with us, by cardinal numbers; yet in that case they take the opposite order— units, tens, hundreds, thousands. Thus, The year 1823, is, Sene Θelêθ wa ᵀuxrien wa θemân mieya wa ʿelf. No article is added to Sene (year), and the numerals of the units must be put in the feminine, as agreeing with Sene. For the dates of *days* they generally use cardinal numbers without the article, since the name of the month serves for the complement. Thus : Fie arbaᵀat Ḥazierân waȜalni mectoub, têriekoh kams'teᵀxar Eiyâr, on 4 of June reached me a letter, its date 15 of May.—Here the numerals are masculine, because the masculine word *yeum*, day, is understood."

§ 9. PLURALS OF NOUNS AND ADJECTIVES.

83. In Art. 78 eight leading types of the imperfect plural were registered. Participles, while used strictly as such, make a perfect plural; masculine in *ien* (*oun*), feminine in in *êt*. For the *first* plural type, I place this masculine perfect plural; for the *second* the perfect feminine. When an adjective is used as a substantive, it sometimes employs the plural *ien* for persons, or *êt* for things; thus from Kair (Kaiyir), good, Kairât, good things. Nouns expressing tradesmen, of the type QaȜȜâb, butcher; make the plural in *ien* (*oun*). According to classical rule, final *n* should drop away, if the word become the leading noun of a compound;

but (it seems) the modern tongue retains this *n* of the plural, though it always drops *n* of the dual; as, Kabbâzien Bafdâd, the bakers of Bagdad ; but, Kabbâzei el Xaifa, the two bakers of the village.

84. To the 2nd type of plurals, in *ét*, *át*, belong—1. Many feminines in *-a*, *-e*. 2. Gerunds of the derived forms of the verb, to be hereafter named. 3. Numerous foreign nouns, without regard to gender or termination. 4. Native feminines in *-a'*, *á;* which make plurals in ayêt, awêt. To the last type conform Turkish words in *á;* as Pâxâ, *pl.* Pâxâwêt; Afâ, *pl.* Afâwêt; Kordâ, small ware, *pl.* Kordâwêt. 5. Nearly all DIMINUTIVE NOUNS, of the form Colaib, a little dog; Xowaiya, a little thing; Mowaiya, a sup of water.

85. The 3rd type (Josour, Xomous) is extremely prevalent with nouns, but not with adjectives. The commonest adjectival type is the 5th (Rijâl, Cibâr), though the 4th, 6th, 7th, and 8th are also adjectival. Plural adjectives are rarely heard except in concord with *rational agents*, and especially in high style are then appropriate; as, El dowal el cibâr, the great Powers; El wozerâ el Tuʒâm, the chief viziers. But in successive pages Faris uses, as if at pleasure, El Haiwânêt el cibâr wa el Sufâr; El Haiwanêt el cebiera wa el Safiera, the animals great and little.

86. A small number of adjectives form a peculiar plural:

Marieʎ, sick, *pl.* Marʎa'.
Qatiel, slain, *pl.* Qatla'.
Jariek, wounded, *pl.* Jarha.
Helic, perishing, *pl.* Helee'.

'Esier, captive, *pl.* 'Esra (as well as 'Oserâ).
Maiyit, dead, *pl.* Maute'.
Ahmaq, silly, *pl.* Hamqa'.

87. The plurals of the following nouns are specially irregular:

Father, abou, ab, *pl.* abâ.
Son, ibn, *pl.* abnâ, benie'.
Brother, akou, ak, *pl.* akâ, akwa.

Mother, omm, *pl.* ommehêt.
Daughter, Girl, bint, *pl.* binêt.
Sister, okt, *pl.* akawêt.
Water, mây, *pl.* miyâh, emwâh.

88. We may treat the "short plural," or tenth type, as regular, when it preserves the vowels of the singular, merely transposing the second; as, Mille, a religious sect, *pl.* Milel; Qobba, a vault, cupola, *pl.* Qobab. But the singular is often of the form Qazên, Luḥâf, or Mediena; in which case the vowels of the plural are *o, o*; as, Loḥof, Modon.

89. Allowance must be made for euphony, especially with the weak consonants ᶜ, w, y. Observe that Ceᶜs, a cup, *pl.* Coᶜous; Raᶜs, *pl.* Roᶜous, are of the third type. Daula, *pl.* Dowal, is of the tenth; Dăwal being converted into Dowal by the *w*.

90. We proceed to speak of the MODERN PLURAL, which is very regular and very important. It applies to all nouns which have *four* or more *strong consonants*, except when their plural is perfect.

Menzil, a lodging.
Bandar, a naval mart.
Kinzier, a pig.

Kandaq, a moat.
Doldol, a hedgehog.
Nomnoma, a wren.

To form the plural insert *á* (*é*) after the second consonant; take *a* (*e*) for your first vowel, and *i, ie* (*u, ui*) for your last, and you have the plurals Menêzil, Banâdir, Kanêzier, Kanâdiq, Dalâdil, Namânim. If the vowel of the singular preceding the last consonant be *á* or *ou*, it becomes *ie* in the plural. Thus (with accent on last syllable of the plurals):

Miklâb, a claw, *pl.* Makâliéb.
Tennour, iron forge, *pl.* Tenâniér.
XakToura, a barge, *pl.* XakâTúir.
Cercedân, rhinoceros, *pl.* Cerâcedién.
QarqaIöun, polecat, *pl.* QarâqaIúin.

91. In a large number of nouns *ʿ*, *w*, or *y* are *counted as true consonants* for this process; especially in those which end in *i* (*y*), as Tabsi(y), a metal saucer, *pl.* Tabêsi(y). So too Zeuraq, a shallop, ГaiTal, a great forest; treated as Zewraq, ГayTal, make plurals Zewâriq, ГayâTul. YaHmour, a nylghau, ʿUsbaT, a finger, Madwad, a manger, similarly give plurals YaHâmiér, ʿEsâbiT, Madâwid. In Cowâra, a hive or comb, Menâra, a lighthouse or spire, *pl.* Cowâyir, Menâyir, perhaps *á* has been treated as *aʿ*. Many nouns of the type Гadier, a pool, Jeziera, an island, follow this law; the *ie* being identical with *iy*; whence *pl.* Гadâyir, Jezêyir, so written in classical books, but, it seems, pronounced Гadâ-iér, Jezê-iér, with accent on the last; which indeed gives the simplest theory, assimilating them to Kanzier, *pl.* Kanâziér. Perhaps Cowâ-iér, Menâ-iér, are also to be thus accented.

BoHaira, a lake, being a diminutive noun from BaHr, sea, should have its plural in *ét*; but we meet BaHâyir (or BaHâ-iér?) as the plural.

92. There is also a large class of nouns with *á* (*é*) in the FIRST syllable of the singular, in which we must first interpret *á* into *aʿ*; next, after deriving hereby the modern plural, we must euphonically change aʿâ or aʿê into awâ, awê. Thus from Sâri(y), a mast, *pl.* Sawâri(y); Bâqiya,

remnant, *pl.* Bawâqi; and even ʿÊniya (ʿEʾniya), a vessel, *pl.* ʿEwêni.

93. It is not always possible to foretell when a noun which has not so many as four strong consonants will form its plural by this law; but when a feminine in -*a* does not form the perfect plural, and is of one of the types Ganiema, Menâra, Fâcihe, Kabiya, the strong presumption is that it will take the modern plural Ganâyim, Menâyir, Fawêcih, Kawâbi. Mediena, a city, Sefiena, a ship, beside the old plurals Modon, Sofon, of the tenth type, have the modern plurals Medâyin, Sefâyin.

In some we may be deceived by a noun of unity. Thus, △obâba, a fly, might suggest a plural △obâyib. But it is a noun of unity, and △obâb means Flies collectively.

94. Some words, expressing tradesmen, take the Turkish termination -*ji*; as, Ṭaubji, cannoneer; Bellaurji, dealer in fine glass; Bostênji, gardener. All such make their plurals in -*jieya*. Besides, there is a third form, purely Arabic, in -*iey* (properly the adjective of relation), as Fakouriey, a seller of pottery; Joukiey, a woollen draper; Soyoufiey, sword cutler. Words of this form, whether substantive or adjective, make their only plural in -*ieya*.

N.B.—Many nouns take two or more plurals, sometimes with a difference of sense; often one is more old-fashioned or of higher style than the other. The English *brothers* and *brethren* will suffice to impress this. Dictionaries give indiscriminately Boḥour, Abḥâr, Biḥâr, seas; Toloul, Etlêl, Tilêl, hills, etc.; and it is often difficult to know which best suits the pitch of the style. Modern use will at last fix on one as suitable for daily life.

§ 10. COMPARATIVES.

95. In Arabic, as in French, the same word is Comparative and Superlative; in fact it has the three senses which we express by "Great*er*, Great*est*, *Very* great." At other times they evade the comparative, as, by saying "Great *above* me," for "Greater than I."

Comparatives are of the type Aħsen, Ecbar, but they are not declined like the adjectives of Colour, Art. 12. E⁵kir (last) is in sense a superlative, but in form is a participle.

96. *Than* after the comparative is expressed by Min; hence after the superlative the partitive Of is generally omitted; as, Aħsen el kail, the finest (of) the horses. The following examples are instructive:

Lem yablof, min el ⱦömr, ecθer min arbaⱦuin ⱦâman,
   He did not attain, *of* age, more *than* forty years.
Mâᴧe faⱦalt, ecθer min el e⁵kar, min el̦ xarr?
   What did I do, more *than* the other, *of* mischief?
El kalâȿ min el̦ ᴧonoub wa el jarâyim hou aⱦʒam min el kalâȿ min el belâyâ,
   Deliverance *from* faults and offences is grander *than* deliverance *from* miseries.
Aqȿa' ⁵erᴧ Muȿr, Furthest (of) the land (of) Egypt.
Anfaⱦ jemieⱦ el ħaiwanât, wa ajdarhe bil molâħaʒa,
   Most useful of all the animals, and most worthy *of them*
      to be noticed.
El awwal aqwa' min el̦ θèni, wa el mauloud min homâ afᴧalhomâ,
   The first (is) stronger *than* the second, and the progeny *from* the two (is) *better than both.*—(Faris.)

El moqâtelât se-tcʿkoʌ hieya aͭʒam min el jidd wa el ḥamâse,
The battles will assume a grander mien *of* earnestness and
energy.—(*Beirout Newspaper*, Ḥad. el Ak.)

In the last, Min for *Of*, immediately after the comparative,
is striking. We might indeed have expected Aͭʒam hieya;
so as to bring "hieya min" side by side. Minnoh, Minneho,
often mean, "than it (is)." Thus: Inna hêʌe el ieyal, leho
mixya, axbeh bil herwela, *minnehe* biḷ racʌ, as for this stag,
to it (is) a gait, liker (more like) to a scamper (amble), *than
it is* to a gallop.

97. The absolute superlative forms a rare feminine, as
Cobra', very great; Ṭoʒma', very mighty. Some make a
plural in -*ien*, as Aqdamien, very ancient; Afʌalien, very
excellent. Others make a substantival plural, of the type
Ecêbir, grandees.

The superlative is generally indeclinable and may precede
its noun, as Aḥsen rajol, best man, very good man. But
Auwal yeum, the first day, and El yeum el auwal, are alike
good. Auwal has a feminine ʿOula' (comparable to Cobra';
also to ʿOkra', other) which is used when it *follows* its feminine noun; as, Eḷ senet el oula', the first year; or Auwal
sene.

In some other phrases (which apparently imitate Turkish
idiom) a common adjective precedes its noun and becomes
indeclinable. The formula, Ṭaziez cotobcom, your valued
letters, is often quoted. In Faris (Nat. Hist.) such phrases
as Ṭaʒuim kiffatoh, his immense swiftness: Ximâliey baḥr
Eurôpâ, the North Sea of Europe; are not seldom met.
Whether this is an improvement to the language, or the very
opposite, learned natives themselves must settle. But with

the superlative the order is normal: as Bi aîla' ʾsautihom, with their highest voice. To the same head we must refer, Bi eʿkir nesmat ḥayâti, with the last breath of my life.

98. Many adjectives do not form a comparative of the type Aḣsen; and their comparative needs to be paraphrased, nearly as in English, by Ecbar (greater), Ecθar (more), or some other familiar comparative, which becomes auxiliary. This is ordinarily done by making a noun the complement, as in Art. 14. Thus:

Ecθar iktilâfan (*or* teſayyoran), more diverse.
Ecθar wojoudan, more as to existence, more numerous.
Axadd qouwaten, more intense as to strength, stronger.
Arda' ſaxmaraten, worse as to fierceness, fiercer.

But this adverbial case of the noun is not in popular style.

§ 11. RELATIVE PRONOUNS.

99. Relatives in most languages are developed partly out of the interrogatives and partly out of the demonstratives. So in Arabic the interrogatives Mán, Má, may be used, not only for Who? What? but also for He-who, That-which. Nevertheless, in modern style they are limited to the *indefinite* relatives Whoever, Whatever. In this use, Mă may be regarded as leaning on the verb, or on the substitute of the verb; thus, Mă-fât, what is past = the past; Mă bain, what is between; Mă-jára, what has happened; Mă-kâlâ, what is vacant; Mă-qolt, what thou saidest. These cohere as one word. In speech, the accent will probably distinguish this Mă from Mâ, not; as, Mâ kâlâ, it is not vacant; Mâ qolt,

thou didst not say. But, Má qolt? what didst thou say? is pronounced exactly as Mâ qolt. This is a grave inconvenience, to avoid which, the moderns wisely prefer to use Mâᴀe (quidnam) in preference to Má, quid?

100. Compounding Man, Mă with Eiy, which? or Coll, all; we have (with verb Cên, was):

Eiyo-man, Eiyoman cên, whatsoever (qui que ce *soit*).
Eiyo-ma, Eiyoma cên, whatsoever.

For which last, more vulgarly, Eix' ma, Eix' ma cên.

Also without Mă, Eiyo becomes relative before a noun, if cên follow; as, Bi eiyo sitr cên, at (any) whatsoever price.

So Colloman, whosoever; Colloma, whatsoever. But Collama is also adverbial, meaning "However much" (*quanto, quantum*), or, in proportion as.

101. The pronoun Léᴀi is relative, and nothing else; but unfortunately it must have the article El before it, and, except when it is nominative to the verb, it needs a pronoun suffix as complement, whence elaborate confusion. Thus, El leᴀi ṭaraf-oh, means either, *Who knew him* (qui noverat eum), or, *Whom he knew* (quem noverat). To get the latter sense we have to render it, "*Who*, he knew *him*," and then imagine Who—him incorporated into Whom. This is one of the grave defects of the language; for as soon as a sentence assumes even moderate complexity, the syntax is apt to be highly uncertain. Léᴀi is declined thus:

| El leᴀi, le quel. | El leᴀien, les quelles. |
| El leti, la quelle. | El lewêt(i), Ellêti, les quelles. |

There is also a classical dual, Elletên, Elletein, abs. and obl.

of both genders. Also, Elléᴧi may be used of both genders and numbers, and is vulgarly shortened into Elli.

The logical complement to Léᴧi is sometimes placed close to it, with much advantage to clearness, when a preposition goes with it; as El leᴧi bihi, by whom; El leᴧi ťandoh, with whom. Leᴧi cannot be preceded by a preposition of its own.

102. El leᴧi cannot be used when it limits its antecedent, but only when the *whole* antecedent is affected by it: as, The man who is present, El̦ rajol, el leᴧi ĥâᴁur. It cannot always be used, even when the antecedent has the English article The; for instance, after the word All, or with a superlative. Thus, "He gave up all *the* money which he had," means, "Whatsoever of money he had;" and "whatsoever" cannot be rendered by El leᴧi. If we express it by Mă, we must transpose, so that Mă may immediately precede its verb: thus, "Sellem mă cên liho min el̦ darâhim." Again: "*The first* man *whom* I saw, appears to us fully defined; for it means, "That individual, whom I saw first of men," illum quem primum vidi. Yet (say the grammarians) the relative clause here *qualifies* the antecedent, which is true (so the Latins throw the verb into the subjunctive: primus homo quem vide*rim*): on this ground El leᴧi is illegitimate. Yet the adverbial relative Enna (that) is here admissible; Awwal rajol *enni* raʿcit-oh (the) first man (*that*) I saw (Faris and Rob. Cr.). So Mă is often used after the superlative; as, Hie afkar mă yoʿsnaʿt, these (are) the finest *that* are made.

The pronominal complement to El leᴧi is not unfrequently suppressed (says Wright) when the sense is clear without it. But his examples show great obscurity resulting.

103. El leʌi begins its own clause, and can have no noun with it. When its antecedent is *understood*, a preposition before El leʌi may belong to the antecedent, as, Li el leʌi— to (the man) who—. We may then regard El as the pronoun *him* (Li, *to;* El, *him;* Leʌi, *who*, etc.). But, even when the antecedent is expressed, and takes El, the Arabs treat it as undefined, if *the* is changeable into *a*. Thus, " The man who is able," may mean, " *A* man, *Any* man who is able;" in that case they omit the word *Who*, or even put the demonstrative Hou (he) for it.

Thus, in general, pronouns of the third person serve for relatives when the antecedent is undefined; as, ʕandi ʃabi, *leho* marɑ̄, in my house is a boy, *to whom* (is) a disease; ʕandi Ḣuʃân, mâ *hou* liya, in my possession (is) a horse, *who* (is) not mine; Dâr, fie*he* jonaina, a house, in *which* (is) a garden. The simultaneous deficiency of the verb " to be" and of the relative is peculiarly unhappy.

104. An astonishingly barbarous syntax is the use of a finite verb for a participle or verbal adjective, the relative pronoun being understood before it. Thus, Rajol yobʃur, is good Arabic for " a man discerns;" yet it is *also* grammatically correct for " a man *who* discerns, *i.e.* a discerning man." This is especially common with the passive verb to supply our verbals in *-ble, -ive, -ate*, etc. When they are also negative, lâ (not) with the verb almost makes a compound adjective. Thus, Belâyâ lâ-yoḣʃa', miseries *innumerable* (viz. *which* are not counted); lâ-yoʕlab, invincible.

105. The adverbial relatives *when, where* . . . . must be paraphrased, if they have some other antecedent than *then, there* . . . . Thus, for " The country *where* I was residing,"

you must say, *in which:* that is, "The country, *which* (el leti) I was residing *in it.*" Again: for "A place *where* there were stones," say, "A place, *in it* stones," mecên, fiehi ḥujâr.

106. In Mă-cên, noticed above, the verb Cên appears indeclinable, but Mă yecoun is also common, as, Eix' ma yecoun (Eiyoma yecoun), be it what it may. After superlatives we may often render Ma yecoun, by the word *possible;* as, AḤsen ma yecoun, the best possible.

107. *Mă* also becomes adverbial in the sense of *While, So long as;* thus, Mă damt Ḥaiyan, so long as I remain alive; but Mă-dâm, more distinctly expresses the sense *While* before another verb. Mă is otherwise an important element of indeclinable relatives; as in Baʕdama, after (apres *que*), Qablama (avant *que*, ante *quam*), Einama, Ḥaiθoma, wheresoever; from prepositions Baʕd, Qabl, and from Ein? where? Ḥaiθ, where. [In modern literature, Ḥaiθoma appears, contrary to classical usage, for *where*, in passages which reject the sense *wherever*. What is gained by this innovation, is not clear. It seems a pity to confound Ḥaiθ and Ḥaiθoma.] So Ṭandama, Waqtima, Ḥuinima, at the moment that, whenever, Ceifama, however. Ṭoulama, as long as. Nay, *verbs* enter such compounds, as, Ṭâlama, it is long that, it is long since; Qallama, it is rare that; Ceθ'rama, it is frequent that; but these (immediately before another verb) are virtually equivalent to the *adverbs* Long ago, Seldom, Often. So with the superlatives, Aqallama, (it is) *very* rare that; Ecθ'rama, it is *very* frequent that.

In place of Ma, sometimes En (that) is found; as, Baʕd en, after (postquam); Ila' en, Ḥatte' en, until; Ḥaiθ en, in case that, before verbs.

§ 12. ELEMENTS OF THE VERB.

108. We begin with the verbs, Ijlis, sit thou : Zekrif, decorate thou.

There are three cardinal tenses, the Imperative (mood), the Aorist, and the Perfect. We omit at present the Dual and the Plurals Feminine, which are rarely used.

IMPERATIVE.

m.s. ijlis	*f.s.* ijlisi	*pl.* ijlisou
m.s. zekrif	*f.s.* zekrifi	*pl.* zekrifou

AORIST.

	1.	2.	3 *m.*	3 *f.*
s.	ajlis	tejlis(i)	yejlis	tejlis
	ozekrif	tozekrif(i)	yozekrif	tozekrif
pl.	nejlis	tejlisou(n)	3. yejlisoun(n)	
	nozekrif	tozekrifou(n)	yozekrifou(n)	

PERFECT.

	1.	2.	3 *m.*	3 *f.*
s.	jelest	jelest(i)	jeles	jeleset
	zekraft	zekraft(i)	zekraf	zekrafet
pl.	jelesna	jelestom(ou)	3. jelesou	
	zekrafna	zekraftom(ou)	zekrafou	

There is no difference in the inflections of the two verbs, except that Zekrif takes *o* for the first letter of its aorist. The *i* in parenthesis for the 2nd pers. sing. denotes the *feminine*. N.B.—In old Arabic the perfect singular had final vowels, thus,

1. jelest*o* ; 2 *m.* jelest*e* ; 3 *m.* jeles*e*.

The final vowels may be kept before a suffix; nay, perhaps we can thus distinguish Baláfna (*we* have arrived or attained) from Balafa-na (or Bal'fa-na), *it* has reached *us*. Faris occasionally writes the 2nd *m.* as Jelest*e*, even without a suffix. To retain this final vowel discriminates 2nd person from 1st, and involves no countervailing evil.

To distinguish the person of Jelest we may add Ana (I) or Ente (thou); but it is often done more delicately by a suffix, if Enna or Lecinna precedes; as, Enn*ee* jelest, that *thou* hast sat; Lecinn*i* jelest, yet I have sat.

Knowing the imperative (as Ijlis, Zekrif) we can inflect the three tenses as above; observing, as to the vowels, only these simple rules:

(*a.*) The vowels of the perfect in the spoken language are always "Fathite," as in the Table, in verbs of such type.

(*b.*) The last vowel of the aorist *is always that of the imperative;* the other vowels as in the Table. The last vowel may be *a, i, o,* in a triradical verb, but invariable in the quadriradical.

(*c.*) If the vowel be *a, i,* the first vowel of the imperative is *i;* but if *o* then *o:* as, Ijlis, sit thou; IqTaT, cut thou; Okroj, go out; OrboT, tie, bind.

The ancient verb distinguished in the aorist *two moods* by a different vowel *o a* added to the end. But this is totally lost and irrecoverable.

109. The classical dual in 2nd and 3rd person is sometimes used. Final *á, é,* is its mark.

IMPER.—2. ijlisê.

AOR.—2. tejlisê(n), 3 *m.* yejlisê(n), 3 *f.* tejlisê(n), as 2nd pers.

PERF.—2. jelestomâ, 3 *m.* jelesê, 3 *f.* jelestê.

The plurals feminine with the old vowels involve much

confusion. When now used, it is with a slight change, apparently as follows (-on, for hon, honna, is the element):

IMPER.—2 *f. pl.* ijlísn *or* ijlíson.

AOR.—2 *f. pl.* tejlísn, tejlíson; 3 *f. pl.* yejlísn, yejlíson.

PERF.—2 *f. pl.* jeléston, 3 *f. pl.* jéleson.

110. A verb like Mrr (*Imperative* Morr), with second and third radical the same, is called SURD. It has a slight irregularity in the modern perfect.

PERFECT.

marart	marart(i)	marr, 3 *m.*	marrat, 3 *f.*
marrait	marraiti		
mararna	marartom	marrou	
marraina	marraitom		

The forms Marrait, Marraina, etc., hurtfully confound the root Mrr with Mry. They will perhaps be driven out by cultivation of the language.

111. When the second radical is *w* or *y*, the verb is called Concave or HOLLOW, as in the Types Qoum, Sier. The aorist and imperative have then no irregularity. But in the perfect the long vowels *ou, ie*, are shortened in *o, i*, before two consonants in 1st and 2nd person; making Qomt, Qomti, Qomna, Qomtom; Sirt, Sirti, Sirna, Sirtom. Also in the 3rd person singular and plural the long vowel of both becomes *â, é*; Qâm, Qâmat, Qâmou; Sêr, Sêrat, Sêrou. The popular imperatives Qoum, Sier, most legitimately supersede Qom, Sir, which rest on an exploded law of euphony.

The two hollow verbs Coun (be), Ꙃuir (become), deserve chief attention.

Be thou, Coun, *f.* Couni, *pl.* Counou.

Shall be, { 1. Ecoun, 2. Tecoun(i), 3. Yecoun, tecoun. (*s.*)
{ 1. Necoun, 2. Tecounou(n), 3. Yecounou(n). (*p.*)

Was, { 1. Cont, 2. Cont(i), 3. Cên, cênet. (*s.*)
{ 2. Conna, 2. Contom, 3. Cênou. (*p.*)

Become thou, Ꞩuir, *f.* Ꞩuiri, *pl.* Ꞩuirou.

Shall { 1. AꞨuir, 2. TaꞨuir(i), 3. YaꞨuir, taꞨuir. (*s.*)
become, { 1. NaꞨuir, 2. TaꞨuirou(n), 3. YaꞨuirou(n). (*p.*)

Have { 1. Ꞩurt, 2. Ꞩurt(i), 3. Ꞩâr, Ꞩârat.
become, { 1. Ꞩurna, 2. Ꞩurtom, 3. Ꞩârou.

Some hollow verbs have *â* in the aorist; as,

	GERUND.	IMPER.	AOR.	PERFECT.
Sleep	Naum	Nâm	Enâm	Nimt, Nâm
Fear	Kauf	Kâf	Akâf	Kift, Kâf
Dread	Heiba	Hêb	Ehêb	Hibt, Hêb

112. The *Perfect* Tense is (on the whole) best rendered by the English "Compound past" or "Present past," as, Jelest, I *have* sat; but we need to render it "I sat," if the context shows historical time to be intended. Also, after In or Iᴧe, *If,* it means *future* perfect; nearly as in English we say, When you *have* done, After you *have* done, for, When you *shall have* done, etc. In this case the verb of response (classically) is also in the Perfect, though we render it as Present Time. The moderns prefer to say Incên, *if,* and then adopt our idiom as to tenses.

113. The Aorist has immense latitude. First and chiefly, it supplies the whole subjunctive mood; but in this sense the final *n* is always dropped from 2nd or 3rd plural. The

particle Li (for) prefixed to the aorist, in good style, suffices to make it *Hortative*, as, Li ejlis! let me sit! Li yejlis! let him sit; and supplies this deficiency of the imperative. On the contrary, Lâ (not) with 2nd or 3rd plural in the spoken tongue uniformly expresses *Prohibition*, like Latin Ne with subjunctive; as, Lâ tejlis! do not sit! Lâ yesier! let him not proceed! Lâ, Mâ, cannot be joined with the imperative.

114. The aorist is also indicative. After Lem (not) it expresses *past* time; as, Lem ejlis, I did not sit, I have not sat; which is apt to be very perplexing. It may in general express Present, Past, or Future, nearly as the Latin present tense in poetry, or in vivid narrative and prophecy, the context alone suggesting the time intended. It is often simply Present, as, Oried, I will, I wish; Lâ oried, Mâ oried, I do not choose. Lem, Lâ, Len, in classical rule, make the aorist Past, Present, Future; but Lâ yejlis, sitt*eth* not; Len yejlis, will not sit, shall not sit, appear to be "high style."

115. To define Future time sharply the simplest method is that of prefixing *Se* to the aorist, which modern literature decidedly adopts: as, Se-yejlis, he will sit; Se-yemorr, he will pass. This too is perhaps high style. On Auxiliaries we shall speak below. Futurity is often denoted beyond question by the context; as, "I go to-morrow," *i.e.* "I *shall* go to-morrow."

But again, *In lem* ejlis, if I *shall not have* sat, recovers for us futurity, as with, In jelest, if I *shall have* sat.

116. The participles have little irregularity. They make *fem. sing.* in -a, -e; *m. pl.* in -ien, -uin (-oun); *f. pl.* in -êt, -ât. The *active* participle of the types Ijlis, Ixrab (drink),

Xien (sully), Loum (blame), is, Jêlis, Xârib, Xâyin, Lâyim; the radical *w* being merged in *y* in the last.

The *passive* of the same types (when the sense admits a passive) is Maxroub, drunk up; Maxien, sullied; Maloum (for Maxyoun, Malwoum), blamed. The surd verb is regular in the passive participle, as, Mesdoud; but the active participle is generally contracted; as, Mârr for Mârir; Ḣadd for Ḣadid. The quadriradical verb has participles, *act.* Mozekrif; *pass.* Mozekraf.

117. An active participle, with *am, art, is, are,* understood, supplies the present indicative of the verb. But if the nominative be then a pronoun, it must be expressed: as, Ana râḋu, I am well satisfied; Houa râyiḣ, he (is) going. Also in this use, the plural of the participle is legitimately in *-oun,* rather than *-ien;* and even in speech one hears *-oun*. Thus, Hel entom rêciboun? are you riding?

118. If the word *while* is added to a participle in English, the Arabs express it by *wa hou* (and he), or *wa hom, wa ana,* etc.; in which case also the plural in *-oun* is preferable. Thus, He sleeps while walking, Yenêm wa hou mâxi. They sleep while walking, Yenêmou(n) wa hom mâxiy*oun*.

119. But if *wa hou, wa ana,* etc., is not inserted, and the active participle singular is in *apposition* to the nominative of the verb, it assumes the adverbial state, by adding *-an, -en;* as, He came riding, Jâ rêciban; or, if the participle be plural, it will take the form *-ien,* not *-oun;* as, Jâʾou rêcibien, they came riding.

120. In fact, *wa hou, wa ana,* etc., with the participle, express our *while* with the verb, even when the preceding verb has a different nominative: as, Dakal beiti, wa ana

nâyim, he entered my house, *while I* (*was*) sleeping; or with the plural, Dakal beitna, wa naḫne nâyimoun, *while we* (were) sleeping.

121. The Arab gerund often (like our own) does duty for an infinitive; but in the spoken language it is generally evaded, as by the modern Greeks, who have replaced it by the subjunctive. Thus, for, Dost thou wish to drink water? a Latin might say, Visne *bibas* aquam? instead of, Visne *bibere* aquam? and an Arab says, Hel toried (en) texrab mây? No word must interpose between En (that) and its verb; hence when En is dropped, the verb (texrab) leads the clause. Dost thou wish the boy to go? is: Hel toried yarouḫ el ʿsabi? not, El ʿsabi yarouḫ.

When the student has reached this point in the grammar, he is at a stage in which a large mass of the language may be picked up. He is recommended to proceed at once to the Third Part (*Praxis*), and turn back only when occasion suggests, to that which we have to add concerning Grammar. In fact, every learner of any language will be wise to do as children do. Let him, with the smallest grammatical apparatus, accumulate the largest possible acquaintance with popular words. Let him combine them as often as possible in the simplest ways; and postpone all intricacies of syntax, and all delicate inquiries, until he is very familiar with the material.

§ 13. TYPES OF THE NOUN.

122. Many nouns are derived from verbs, some verbs from nouns. We have already observed—1. A noun of unity, ending in -*a*, -*e;* and 2. a diminutive of the types Colaib

(little dog), Boḣaira (little sea, lake). 3. A noun of place or time has the type of Mafrab or Mafrib, the west, place or time of sunset: so Maṯlaf, hayrack; Maqʃab, canebrake; or with feminine ending, Mabṯaka, a melon bed; Mesbaʕa, a place of wild beasts; from Baṯuik, melon; Seboʕ, wild beast. 4. The noun of instrument differs from the last in having *i* for its first vowel; it also sometimes elongates its second vowel into *á*. Thus, Minfak, bellows; Mijmara, brazier; Miftêḣ, key; Miqlâya, frying pan. Many of these, numbered 3 and 4, are *verbal* nouns.

Abstract nouns may sometimes be regarded either as gerunds of verbs, or as related to an adjective; in some cases the two are distinguished by a vowel. 5. The active gerund has very often the type Kaʕf, carrying off; Kalq, creating; Δarb, a beating. 6. A noun of unity from this has the type Δarba, a single blow.

7. So Sefar, travelling; Faraḣ, rejoicing, gladness. 8. Hence the noun of unity, Sefara, a voyage.

9. The abstract nouns, Cibr, greatness; Cobr, grandeur; Ʒufr, smallness; Ʒöfr, contemning, contempt (if indeed this vocalization be right), are related to the adjectives Cebier, Ʒafier; so Rokʃ, cheapness, to Rakieʃ; Somn, fatness, to Semien. Also in the feminine form, Sorʕa, quickness, with Serieʕ; Boʕda, distance, farness, with Baʕuid. 10. Ciθra, plenty, is the abstract to Ceθier, much; but this type is commonest when the root is *surd*. Thus, Qilla, deficiency, with Qaliel; Riqqa, thinness, with Raqieq; Xidda, intensity, with Xadied; Liᴧᴧe, deliciousness, with Leᴧieᴧ. 11. From *hollow* verbs come such as Ṯoul, length, with Ṯawiel; and in feminine, Jouda, goodness.

12. With neuter verbs, Jolous (sitting), is a common gerundial type. 13. Not less common is the type Sohoula, case, both for abstract nouns and for the gerund of neuter verbs. 14. Citêba, writing, is again gerundial. 15. Nearly the same is the type Najâba, nobleness, extremely common for abstract nouns. 16. Raᴀiele, vileness, is a somewhat rarer type. In El kaziena, the treasury; El Kaliefa, the Caliph, it is concrete.

123. In a tabular view they stand thus:

TYPES OF NOUNS.

1. kobz-e
2. colaib
    boḧaira
3. mafrab
    mabʼaka
4. minfak
    miklâb
    mijmara
    miqlâya
	5. Ẋarb
	6. Ẋarba
	7. sefar
	8. sefara
	9. cibr
	    cobr
	    sorʼa
	10. ciθra
	    qilla
		11. ʼoul, ʼuib
		    jouda
		12. jolous
		13. sohoula
		14. citêba
		15. najâba
		16. raᴀiele

The commonest *gerunds* (of the primary "triliteral" verb) are of the types Naʒr, Jolous, Faraḧ, Citêba, Sohoule. Of these the two last are like our nouns in *-tion*, and make the plural in *-êt*. Of the rest, Naʒr is the commonest type for active verbs, Jolous and Faraḧ for neuter verbs.

124. Special list of abstract nouns of 15th type, related to adjectives.

Naḧâfa, leanness.
Laṭâfa, gentleness.
Seqâfa, sickliness.
Radâwa, badness.
Wesêka, dirtiness.
Melâḧa, comeliness.
Ƹarâfa, elegance.
Ġalâʓa, uncouthness.
Najâba, nobleness.

Belâda, stupidity.
Ġabâwa, doltishness.
Jehéla, ignorance.
Ƹalâba, solidity.
Ƭaʓâma, mightiness.
Seṭâda, happiness.
Mehêra, skilfulness.
Ḧalâwa, sweetness.
Marâra, bitterness.

Frequently there are two forms; as, Loṭf and Laṭâfa, Seṭâda and Soṭouda, etc.; the same thing happens in most languages. The Dictionary, and not the Grammar, must inform a learner what form of gerund, or of abstract noun, is practically current under each root.

§ 14. AUXILIARY VERBS.

125. LET is expressed by 'Daṭ (more classical) or Kalli (more popular), prefixed to 1st or 3rd person of the aorist; as, 'Daṭ-ni axrab, let me drink (in Latin, *sine me bibam*); Kallieni axouf, let me see; Kalliena nexouf, let us see. Xouf is a popular verb: more classical is, 'Daṭ-ni ara', let me see. But in good style the mere particle Li suffices to express our Let; as, Li yefout, let him pass in. In Syria, they use Tè as a hortative particle (Latin *age*), instead of Li; as, Tè yarouḧ, let him go. [I think that Tè means *come*, being the imperative of the verb ˁEteˁ, *he came*. But De Perceval interprets it as a contraction of Ḧatte, until.]

126. GOING is popularly rendered by Râyiḧ, exactly like English; but in Barbary they say Mâxi, walking. Thus

Faris has, Hel hou râyiḫ en yojaddid el jidâl? Is he going to renew the dispute? (Lit. *en* yojaddid, *ut* renovet, that he should renew.) But this use of Râyiḫ is no more in high style than is Going in English.

127. WILL, expressing purpose, has many substitutes, all of them followed by the aorist, with En (that) often understood. Chiefly; Oried, I wish, I will, I choose; Morâdi en, (it is) my wish that; Qaʽṣdi en, (it is) my design that; or, Ana qâʽṣid, I am designing; Ana ʽâzim, I am resolving; Ana nâwi, I am intending; Ehomm, I meditate.

Faris has, Nâwi temʽṭor, (it is) intending to rain, for, it is *going* to rain.

In Aleppo, Bedd (contracted, it seems, from Bi wedd) is in general use. From Wedd, wish, choice, will; comes Bi weddi, (it is) in my will; Bi weddee, (it is) in thy will, etc. Hence they make,

Beddi arouḫ, I will go; Beddee terouḫ, thou wilt go, etc. This is perhaps confined to Syria. If *Bi wedd* be pronounced in full, it must probably be admissible any where; but the Aleppines use it to express Futurity as well as Will or Wish.

128. For mere FUTURITY, nothing is better than the classical particle *Se-* prefixed to the aorist; which is still living in literature. Thus, Se-yarouḫ, he will go; Se-narouḫ, we shall go; Se-tera', thou shalt see.

At Bagdad, Yecoun (it will be) gives a future notion to the verb; as, Yecoun yarouḫ, he will go; Yecoun râḫ, he will have gone. Yaʽsuir, it will be, may be in like manner employed; as, Yaʽsuir temʽṭor, it will rain.

The verb Ezmaʽṭ, he hastened, or rather the participle, Mozmiʽṭ, hastening, is also current, as follows: Hou mozmiʽṭ yabieṪ, he is hastening to sell, *i.e.* he is *on the point* of selling.

129. CAN, expressing ability, is rendered by Aqdir, I am able; or Ana qâdir; or Liya qodra en, to me (is) power that. Or again, they say, Ana qâbil, I am capable; Liya qâbilieya en, to me (is) capacity that. At Bagdad they say, OṪuiq, or OṪuiq Ṫala en, I have force for; or, Liya Ṫâqa en. (More ordinarily, with a negative, Mâ oṪuiq, or Lâ Ṫâqa liya biᶜen, means, I have no *resisting* power; I cannot withstand *a disease;* I cannot afford *an expense*.) Literati are fond of the strangely obscure word, EsteṪuiṪ, I am able. Worst of all by far is the idiom of Aleppo, which pronounces AḦsen, I am able; apparently meaning OḦsin (ɪᴠth form), I *succeed*. Thus, I do not succeed to do a thing, means, I *cannot*.

For CAN, meaning possibility, you may say Yomcin, it is possible; or participle Momcin; and Emcen, it was possible. Negatively, Lâ yomcin, Mâ momcin, it is not possible; Lem yomcin, it was not possible; Mâ teheyya liya, it was not *at hand* (*in promptu*) for me; or again, MoḦâl, MosteḦuil, impossible, absurd. Also, Lâ yaꝪuḦḦ, it is not sound, virtually means, It cannot be.

It is also in Arabic idiom to say, Lâ telḦaq yedi Ṫala en— My hand does not reach so far that—. More shortly, Leis fie yedi, it is not in my hand, *i.e.* I am not able. In Syria this is cut down into Fieya, it is in me; Mâ fice, it is not in thee, *i.e.* I can, thou canst not.

130. For MAY (of permission) we can use Yejouz, it passes, it is permitted; YaꝪuḦḦ, it is sound; YobâḦ, it is open and free. Also the participles Jâyiz, MobâḦ. Or Yesouf liya, it is allowed me.

Faris exhibits the singular ellipsis, Hel liya en—? is it for me that—? *i.e.* is it *permitted* to me that—. So even in English, It *is* not *for me* to do so and so— (*Non meum est ut—*). But the omission of the verb "to be," as well as the predicate, makes the Arabic ellipsis very harsh.

131. OUGHT admits a like elliptical phrase, Talaiya en, (it rests) on me that. Besides, we can say, Yenbafi, it befits; Yelicq, it beseems; Yejib, it behoves; or Wâjib Talaiya, (it is) a duty on me. Again, Yaḥaqq Talaiya, it is right for me; Yaṣuḥḥ liya, it is proper for me; Yajmol, it is comely, or becoming; Yaqtalu, it is required. The most popular of these is Wâjib Talaiya. Besides we can use Yelzem, Lêzim en, though this rather means Need, necessity.

132. For MUST, two formulas are highly popular. Lâ bodd en, no escape that—; Lâ bodd (en) terouḥ, thou must necessarily go. Next, Lêzim, which originally meant, sticking close, has somewhat degenerated; so that they now say, Lêzimni, it is necessary *for* me, *i.e.* I must, or, I want, I need. This word is greatly overworked by the vulgar.

133. The verb Cên (it was) is also auxiliary in Arabic; not only to make a passive verb, as in English, but to form tenses by its peculiar force of *time*; since Yecoun is essentially future* and Cên is historical time, *i.e.* it *was*, not, it *has been*. Hence we obtain:

Roḥt, I went or have gone.	Arouḥ, I go.
Cên roḥt, I had gone.	Cên arouḥ, ⎫ I went.
Yecoun roḥt, I shall have gone.	Cont arouḥ, ⎭
	Yecoun arouḥ, I shall go, I am to go.

* So De Perceval positively asserts; and it seems, with great reason.

133b. We can hardly class as auxiliary the verbs which express to *begin*, before another verb. These are Ebdi, I open; Eʻkoᴀ, I take; Ajʇal, I set, set to; Axraʇ, I institute; Aʇfoq, I establish; Aꜱuir, I become. All drop a part of their sense to assume the meaning of Begin: the commonest is Ebtedi (in vɪɪɪth form, see 136), whence Ibtedâ, Mobtedâ, a beginning. These verbs are followed by Enna (that, quod, ὅτι) with the aorist *Indicative* of the other verb; not by En (ut, ἵνα) with subjunctive; apparently because an attained result, not a mere intention, is expressed. Thus, The sailors began to howl, Jaʇalou el mellâḣöun yowelwil*oun*; Ibtêdou *or* ꜱârou yaꜱrok*oun*, they began to shout. It is here seen that the particle Enna (that) is readily dropped from the phrase.

Cên roḣt or Cont roḣt, also supplies, I *should have* gone; and Cên arouḣ (Cont arouḣ), I *should* go; under a non-existing hypothesis. The double compounds, Cên yecoun arouḣ, *I was to go*, and Cên yecoun roḣt, *I was to have gone*, are perhaps peculiar to Bagdad; as, Beddi arouḣ, I am to go; Cên beddi arouḣ, or rather Cont beddi arouḣ, I was to go; are Syrian.

§ 15. CLASSES OF THE VERB.

134. Quadriradical verbs, such as Zekrif, have their vowels all fixed, and in the modern language scarcely go beyond the two following Forms, typified by the Imperatives zekrif, tezekraf.

Form.	I.	II.
Imperative	zekrif	tezekraf
Aorist 1 p. s.	ozekrif	etezekraf
Perfect 3 p. s.	zekraf	tezekraf
Gerund	zikrâf	tezekrof
Participle act.	mozekrif	motezekrif
Participle pass.	mozekraf	[motezekraf]?

The learner must use this and such like tables for *reference*, when he meets with a verb of such a class. Until the case occurs, he will not be able to use the table to advantage. The two "*forms*" are often comparable to what we call Voices in Latin and Greek. In fact the IInd is ordinarily either like a Passive or a Reflective ("middle") voice to the I$^{st.}$ In that case there cannot be any passive participle to the IInd form. But the IInd form may be an independent verb. Older Arabic admits of a IIIrd form izka*n*rif, and a IVth izkarfif.

135. Triradical verbs have more numerous forms. Even in the spoken language *ten* must be counted, though no one verbal root possesses them all. To exhibit the types, it is expedient to form all from a single root, *as if* they all existed. The root Bdl, imperative Ibdil (exchange) may represent all the types. In the classical tongue every form except the ixth has its passive distinct from its active; but we confine ourselves to the passive of the first form. The active *first* form alone has the vowel of the aorist doubtful, as also the form of the gerund doubtful, as stated in 108*b*, 122. Its

active participle is also peculiar, not being formed by initial *m*. Any of the forms *may* have a passive participle, even in the spoken language, if the sense of the form itself be that of an active verb. Only the ixth form is *always* a neuter verb, and can have no passive.

When there is a passive participle, it is formed from the active participle (in all forms but the 1st) exactly as in the quadriradicals, by changing *i* of the last syllable into *a*. (This *i* might be *u*, if a coarse consonant were in juxtaposition.)

136. Scheme of the Ten Forms of the Triradical Verb:

	Imperat.	Aor. 1 p. s.	Perf. 3 p. s.	Gerund.	Participle.
i.	ibdil	ábdil	bádal	(badal)	bâdil
Pass.	——	obdal	bódil	——	mabdoul
ii.	baddil	obaddil	baddal	tebdiel(a)	mobaddil
iii.	bâdil	obâdil	bâdal	{ bidâl / mobâdala }	mobâdil
iv.	abdil	obdil	abdal	ibdâl	mobdil
v.	tebaddal	etebaddal	tebaddal	tebaddol	motebaddil
vi.	tebâdal	etebâdal	tebâdal	tebâdol	motebâdil
vii.	inbádil	anbádil	inbádal	inbidâl	monbádil
viii.	ibtédil	abtédil	ibtédal	ibtidâl	mobtédil
ix.	ibdall	abdall	ibdall	ibdilâl	mobdill
x.	istébdil	estébdil	istébdal	istibdâl	mostebdil

The t due to the VIIIth form becomes d after d or z, ⌂ after ⌂, ᛐ after ᛐ, ⵣ, ꝫ, ʒ. Also if ˤ, w, or y, be the first radical it becomes t before t in the VIII$^{th.}$ Thus the root Wel makes Ittécil (for Iwtécil) in VIII.

137. All the gerunds of the derived forms make plural in -ét. The gerund of II. might be tebdiela or tebdila, instead of tebdiel, which is standard. In III. mobâdala is a commoner form than bidâl; but both often co-exist.

It will be seen that III. is formed from II., and VI. from V. (except in the gerund) by the same simple law. After duly understanding this we might drop III. and VI. from the Table. Forms VII. and VIII. are likewise formed by a common law; so that either will suffice as a type.

Form X. is remarkable, *ist* being prefixed to the root. This is explained completely from Coptic, from Zouave, from Assyrian, and from certain traces in Chaldee or Hebrew. A form is in fact *lost*, whose Imperative was *Sebdil;* and from this Istebdil was formed, nearly as VIII. from I. The form Sebdil was a Causative verb, but it is superseded by IV.

The tenses are inflected according to the laws explained in 108. Carefully note the initial o in the aorist of II., III., IV. Observe also that the last vowel is i in the imperative (and aorist) of II., III., IV., VII., VIII., X., but is a in V., VI., IX. Yet in the participle active of all the forms it is i.

138. Any two forms, as Ibdil and Bâdil, are strictly independent verbs, as in Latin fugio and fugo, or sedeo, sido, sedo. In fact sometimes they are as unlike in sense as fero and ferio, condo and condio. Such phenomena are very deceptive. It is *always* safest for the learner to learn nearly every form for itself, as if it were a new verb.

Nevertheless, the IInd or IIIrd being given active verbs, we can positively infer the existence and meaning of the Vth or VIth; for the Vth always is to the IInd and the VIth to the IIIrd its reflective, neuter, or passive. The VIIth, when it exists, is passive to the Ist, if the Ist be active; or else to the IVth.

The IVth is properly causative to the Ist. Hence if the Ist be neuter the IVth is its active. If the Ist be active the IVth has two accusatives.

The VIIIth is comparable to the Greek middle voice, in relation to the Ist, and often supersedes the Ist arbitrarily. In other instances it serves as a true passive to the Ist.

The IInd is (perhaps most properly) frequentative or intensive of the Ist; as, IqTaT, cut; QaTTuT, cut in pieces, chop up; Icsir, break; Cessir, break in pieces. But it is often causative to the Ist, and the modern tendency is to work it entirely in this direction, and nearly supersede the IVth; apparently because vowels are obscurely and corruptly sounded. Yet even when II. and IV. are both causative, the sense sometimes differs, because II. is still frequentative and imperfect. Thus from the root UTlam, know thou, comes II. Tallim, *teach* thou (as a teacher who repeats or causes to repeat); but IV. ATlim, *inform, advertize*, viz., by a complete single act.

The IIIrd is often related to the primitive, as a Latin verb compounded with Con. It almost always governs an accusative, and the syntax differs from that of the Ist. Something *mutual* is ordinarily suggested, often *rivalry*. Thus, Ectob lee, I write to thee, Ocêtib-ee, I *be-write* thee; AqTod, I sit, OqâTud-ee, I sit-with thee; but OqTud-ee, OqaTTud-ee, I seat thee.

The IXth is comparable to a Latin inceptive verb in -esco, and is especially used for verbs of Colour, as erubesco, nigresco.

The Xth often expresses Desire (like a verb in -urio). It also expresses a Judgment; as, I judge a thing small, or great. But sometimes it is a mere neuter verb,—it may be, with a very obscure relation of sense to the primitive: as, Istemarr, he persevered; IsteTâʔ, he was able (from root ʔwʔ); Isteqall, he was plenipotentiary, unrestricted, independent.

The VIth often expresses Pretension or Affectation: as, Tebâha, he made display of finery; Tefâkar, he played the self-glorifier.

The relation of the Vth and VIth to the IInd and IIIrd is obviously the same as that of the IInd to the Ist of Quadriradicals. Also the IIIrd and IVth of Quadriradicals are analogous to the VIIth and IXth of Triradicals.

139. By means of these derived forms, the language is at no loss to express the Passive idea. It is not wonderful then, that the *vocalized* Passives have almost vanished out of the spoken language. None of them had any Imperative or any Gerund. The Aorist was formed by vowels *o, a;* the Perfect by vowels *o, i.* The vocalized Passive of I. is heard popularly in a few words; indeed, is used freely by the newspapers in very unpretending and business-like relations; hence it may be inferred that it will be quite recovered with the progress of literary cultivation. Thus from Octob, write; Oqtol, kill; come passives Cotib, Qotil; Yocteb, Yoqtel.

When the VIIIth is active, it sometimes takes a vocalized passive: thus from Intekib, elect thou; Ontokib, he was elected; Ontekab, I am elected (eligor). Here the Perfect takes *o, o, i*; the Aorist *o, e, a*.

The Passive of III. changes *á* of the Perfect active into *ou*.

§ 16. DEGENERATE VERBS.

140. Triradical verbs degenerate when the second and third radical are the same, or when one or more radical is weak; that is, when it is ʕ, w, or y.

We have seen that the participle of the *Surd* verb undergoes contraction; as Mârr for Mârir, Xâdd for Xâdid. A similar contraction occurs in the IIIrd and VIth forms, but not in the Imperative. Nor indeed can such contraction apply in the Gerund *xidád* of III. The forms II. and V. follow the standard of Ibdil perfectly; so do the imperatives of all forms but I. and X. But it is worth while to present a nearly full table. The words in *Italics* follow the law of Ibdil. No Surd verb has a IXth form.

	IMPER.	AORIST.	PERFECT.	GERUND.	PARTICIPLE.
I.	xodd	axodd	xadd	(xadd)	xâdd
III.	*xádid*	oxâdd	xâdd	{ *xidád* / moxâda }	moxâdd
IV.	*axdid*	oxidd	axadd	*ixdád*	moxidd
VI.	*texádad*	etexâdd	texâdd	texâdd	motexâdd
VII.	*inxádid*	anxadd	inxadd	*inxidád*	mouxadd
VIII.	*ixtédid*	axtedd	ixtedd	*ixtidád*	moxtedd
X.	istexidd	estexidd	istexadd	*istixdád*	mostexidd

The only Passive Participles are the types Maxdoud of I. and Mostexadd of X.

141. *Hollow* verbs are quite regular in II., III., V., VI., IX. (There is *one* such verb in IX. from the root Eswadd, black; hence Moswidd, nigrescens.) Some are regular in IV. as YoLiwij, he necessitates. We saw in the Participle of I. the verb "hollow by *w*" assume *y* instead; the same takes place in the Passive of I. except the participle, and in IV., VII., VIII., X. Thus when a verb in one of these forms is given, we cannot tell by its aspect whether the root has *w* or *y*. The types stand thus: from root Qwl.

	Imper.	Aorist 1.	Perf. 3.	Gerund.	Partic.
I. Pass.	——	oqâl	qiel	——	maqoul
IV.	aqiel	oqiel	aqâl	iqâla	moqiel
VII.	inqal	anqâl	inqâl	inqiyâl	monqâl
VIII.	iqtel	aqtêl	iqtêl	iqtiyâl	moqtêl
X.	isteqiel	esteqiel	isteqâl	istiqâla	mosteqiel

The feminine form of the Gerund in IV. and X. deserves remark.

142. When the 1st radical is *w* or *y*, the verbs are called *Assimilated*. If the verb be *y*, the verb in modern use is all but regular; only after *o* the *y* becomes *u*. If the first radical be *w*, this letter is dropped in the Aorist, according to the best style; as, Wejed, he found; Ejid, I find. But *Surd* verbs of this class treat *w* as a strong radical, as Awodd, I love. We have also said that in VIII. the *wt* becomes *tt*.

143. When the 3rd radical is *w* or *y*, the verbs are called Defective. They are of four classes, as follows: .

1 Aor.	1. afzou	2. armi	3. anse'	4. arʕa'
3 Perf.	faze	rama'	nesi	raʕa'
	maraud	throw	forget	feed cattle

of which the 1st is defective in *w*, the rest in *y*.

In the 2nd and 3rd *pl.* of Aorist, and *pl.* of Imperative, *w* or *y* is clipped out: though in Barbary they say, Termiyou, Yermiyou, for the normal Termou, Yermou.

The perfects are slightly irregular.

1. 2.	Fazeut	Ramait	Nesiet	Raʕait,
3.	Faze, -et	Rama, -met	Nesi,- siyet	etc.
1. *pl.*	Fazeuna	Ramaina	Nesiena	as Rama
2.	Fazeutom	Ramaitom	Nesietom	
3.	Fazeu	Ramau	Nesou	

The Active participle is in all of the type Fâzi(y).

The Passive Participle is Mafzouw, for 1, and Mermiey for 2, 3, 4.

Verbs defective in *w* are few; and in modern use they all tend to supersede *w* by *y*. *In all the derived forms this is done.* Otherwise, these forms have no irregularity, but that *y* falls away after *a*, and *o* becomes *i* before *y*. Thus in the Gerund of v., Terammi(y) for Terammoy. Also, as usual, -*áya* replaces -*áʾa* in feminine participles passive.

A suffix, by changing the accent, introduces *á*, *é*, for *a*, *e*, in 3rd person masculine singular of the perfect.

144. Of verbs "Hamzated" in 1st radical, ꜤekaA (take) is the type. In Imperative of I., initial *i* or *o* is dropped (with Ꜥ); as KoA, take thou; Mor, command; Col, eat thou. After *o* the Ꜥbecomes *w*, as, TowâkiA, for ToꜤâkiA (reprove); hence, vulgarly, in the whole form the Ꜥis apt to become *w*.

Surd verbs of this class take *w* for Ꜥ in their aorist; as, ꜤEnn, he groaned; *Aor.* Awinn. Indeed in modern use *w* has displaced Ꜥ in the whole root ꜤEjj (catch fire, flame out); as, Wejj, *Aor.* Yawijj; and Wejja, a blaze.

145. When Hamze is 2nd radical, as in IsꜤel (ask), the participle is Meswoul for MesꜤoul, a microscopic difference. The only derived form of this whole class (says C. de Perceval) is séyal of III.

146. When Hamze is 3rd radical, the only irregularities are such as obvious euphony suggests. But in popular use these verbs merge their Ꜥ in *y*.

147. Verbs doubly defective are chiefly the following:

a. Jâ, he came; Eji, I come (TeꞮâl, come thou!).—Perf. Jiet, I came; Jât, she came; JaꜤou, they came; Jâyi, coming; Mejie, arrival.—Pass. jie, *ventum est*.

b. ꜤEte, he came; ꜤEtet, she came; Eteit, I came; Etou, they came; Eti, I come; Yètou, they come; Eti, coming; Itiyân, arrival. VIth form, TeꜤête. Imperative TeꜤ (come).

c. XâꜤ, he wished; Xât, she wished; Xiet, I wished; XâꜤou, they wished; Yexâ, he wishes.

d. SâꜤ, he misbehaved; 1. 2. p. Sout. In IV. Esâ, he mismanaged; *Aor.* Osie.

e. ꜤAbaꜤ, he refused; like ꜤEteꜤ.

f. ꜤEyes, he despaired; *Aor.* EꜤwies?

g. Raʸa, he saw; Raʸet, she saw; Raʸeit, I saw; Raʸou, they saw. Ara', I see; Arou, they see. Râ, see thou. *Passive*, Roʸi, it was seen; *Aor.* Yora, it seems, is seen. IV. Orie, I show; Arie, show thou (*vulg.* Arwi, Rawwi). V. Terâʸa liya, it appeared to me, but more popularly, Terâwa. III. Râya, he played the hypocrite (made a show).

ʸEteʸ and Raʸa are both popular words, but not in the physical sense, in which Jâ and Xâf supersede them. ʸEteʸ means, to come as an event; *part.* El ʸêti, the future, venturus. Raʸâ means, he saw with the mind, he judged (Râÿ, opinion), he saw a vision (Rouya, vision). Thus, In raʸeit, if you shall have seen (it good).

---

148. The inability to compound verbs with prepositions is a grave defect in Arabic. In part they supply it by the creation of new roots, in part by detached prepositions (which nevertheless cannot enter derivatives), and in part by a rather arbitrary use of the derived forms. We have seen that the IIIrd is often like a Latin compound of Con; this is but a hint at the practice. The VIIth is sometimes like a Latin compound of Re; and so of others.

Let an Englishman reflect on some of our own verbs, as, Bring up; which, for secondary meanings, has Rear or Educate, Vomit, and (popularly) Pull up, Rein up suddenly, Bring to a sudden stop. If we met some Arabic root interpreted in a dictionary, 1. Educate, 2. Vomit, 3. Check *a horse*, we might think it a monstrosity. This will suffice to indicate how an injudicious lexicographer increases difficulty. In fact, the pupil should, if possible, confine himself for a while to the primary cardinal senses.

149. We are accustomed to form a Passive Participle even from a verb which has a detached preposition; as, from "I *allude to* a thing," "the thing alluded *to*." The Arabs seem to aim at, but miss, this idiom. They cannot bear the preposition isolated; hence they attach to it a superfluous pronoun suffix, in defiance (it might seem) of logic. Thus, from Oumi ileihi, I *hint at* it (nod to it); they get, El xai^z el mouma ilei*hi*, the thing hinted at. This pervades the language.

We may partially explain it by the analogy of the Latin *impersonal* use of the Passive verb; especially since the participle in this idiom has no concord with the preceding noun. Thus, "The slaves above mentioned," "The slaves spoken of," El Ɵabied el maq*oul* Ɵanhom; not, maqouloun or maqoula, though Ɵabied is plural. The concord to Ɵabied is found in the plural *hom;* and Maqoul is impersonal, like Latin Dictum (est) for Diximus. Thus a rude translation might be, *Oi* servi *oi*—dicebatur de iis; *i.e. Oi* servi, *de quibus* dicebatur. And in this idiom the second El is often said to be put for Elleλi, who. In fact, the vocalized passive is occasionally used like the Latin impersonal verb.

§ 17. ADVERBS AND CONJUNCTIONS.

150. Adverbs of Time:

Afterwards, baƟdan; *pop.* baƟdoh.	Already, qad (with Perfect only).
Again, aiλan (see also 153).	Always, dâyiman.

Before (*adv.*) qablan
Beforehand, min qabl.
Daily, yeum bi yeum; yeuman fa yeuman.
Early, beccier.
Earlier and later, sèbiqan wa lâḥuqan.
Ever (with negative), ʿebadan.
For ever, ila el ʿebad.
Formerly, sèbiqan.
Henceforward, min baʿdoh; min elʿân wa ṣaʿudan.
Hereafter, seuf.
Hitherto, ila elʿên.
Instantly, Ḥâlan, fil Ḥâl, fiḷ sêʿa, lil waqt, fil Ḥuin.
Lately, ʿan qarieb [also Soon].
Long ago, ʿâlama (it is long ago that).
No longer (see 153).
Meanwhile, fil eθnâ.
Now, elʿên; hêᴀe el waqt; hêᴀe el sêʿa.
Now and then (at times; occasionally), aḥyânan; Ḥuin fa Ḥuin.
Just now, têwâ (a little while ago, Alep.); bi hêᴀe el qorb.

Often, amrâr ceθiera; coll qaliel; ceθ'rama (it is often that).
Very often, écθarma.
How often? cém marra?
Once, marraten; marraten mà; marra wâḥuda.
Presently, in a minute, marrat ʿokra'.
Rarely, nâdiran; zehiedan?
Quickly, ʿâjilan; serieʿan.
Seldom, qallama (it is seldom that).
Sometimes, aḥyânan; auqât auqât; baʿṭ auqât.
Sometimes — Sometimes; marraten — marraten; têraten — têraten.
Soon, ʿan qarieb [also, Lately]; lâḥuqan, Kaz.(?).
Still, baʿdoh (vulg.?); liḷ sêʿa (see also 153).
Then (at that time), iᴀᴀêc; waqtaʿiᴀin; Ḥuinaʿiᴀin, yeumaʿiᴀin.
To-day, elyeum.
To-morrow, fadan.
Yesterday, ʿems.
Not yet, liḷ sêʿa mâ—liḷ sêʿa lâ—.

151. Adverbs of Quantity:

Almost, illa qaliel, cêd (see 153).
Barely, (bi) mojarrad.
Enough, cefâya(ten).
Entirely, bil collieya.
Few, qaliel(oun).
Gradually, tedriejan, ʕuba-qan ʕan ʕubaq.
Little, qaliel.
A little, xowaiya.
Little by little, xaiˤan fa xaiˤan.
Less, aqall.
In the least, adna' xaiˤ (the slightest thing).

Many, ceθier(oun).
Much, ceθier.
How much? } cêm?
How many? }
How much? qadd eix'?
More, ecθâr.
Nearly, teqrieban.
Only, faqaʕ (vulg. bes).
Scantily, Ɫanien? (Boethor; guère).
Scarcely, ecudan? bil jehd; bil ceid? (See 153).
Somewhat, xaiˤen.
Somewhere about, qadar.
Totally, qâʕuba(ten).

152. Conjunctions governing Verbs:

According as, } cema,
As, } miθlima.
As if, ceˤenna.
Although, } waˤin, walau,
Though, } maʕ en.
Because, liˤenna; bi sebab enna; liˤejl enna.
Before (antequam), qablama.
Not but that, naʕam enna.
Not but that, illa inna (also, Nevertheless; in Faris).

In case,* bi ḥaiθ(en). [Bi ḥaiθ ceᴧê, in such a case as this.]
On condition that, ʕala en, bi xarʕ en.
Except that, } ġair enna.
Only that, }
Forasmuch as, ḥaiθ inna; iᴧ enna (iᴧ iuna?) Rob. Cr. 244.
Inasmuch as, bi ma inna.

---

* Kazimirski says, Bi ḥaiθ en, a tel point que.

On the ground that (as though), ʿala enna.
However (quocunque modo), ceifama.
How much soever, mehma.
How often soever, collama, mehma.
[However, *adv.* = Howbeit, be it as it may, ceifamacên.]
If, in, incên, iᴧe; lau (were it that).
If ever, iᴧma.
Lest, liˤella, liʾeila.
As long as, madâm, ʿoulima, mă.
As much as, qaddama.
Insomuch that, ʿala enna, bi nauʿ ḥatte, (*in sort that*).
O that, yâ laite.
In proportion as, collima, qaddima, ḥasbima, qadrima.
In respect that, min ḥaiθ enna.
Seeing that, Since, naȝaran en, iᴧecên, lemmacên.

Ever since, mouᴧ, moᴧᴧ.
As soon as, ʿandama, auwal ma, ḥâlima, waqtima, ḥuinima.
That (ut, ἵνα), en.
That (ὅτι, quòd), enna.
So that, ḥatte' ˤinna; ʿala enna.
In that, fie ˤenna.
In order that, li, cei, licei, ḥatte.
That not (*ut ne, ἵνα μή*), ella, ceila.
Till, Until, ḥatte, ḥatte en.
Unless, illa, iᴧlem.
Unless it were that, laula.
When, lemma, iᴧ, iᴧe ma (mete'?).
Whenever, iᴧma. [Be it when it may, iᴧ ma cên.]
Where, ḥaiθ.
Whereas, ḥâl inna.
Wherever, ḥaiθoma, einama.
Whilst, bainama, ʿandama, madâm (bima), b'iᴧma, fiema.

153. There is a tendency of the language (shared by Hebrew) to express adverbs of time by verbs; as, by saying, "He *repeated* to go," instead of, "He went again." Thus:

1. Mâ îâd, he did not repeat, degenerated into "not again." Lâ teîoud tefîal-he, do not do it again.

2. "No longer" is expressed by the verb Baqi (it remained over, continued) which changes with the person. Thus: I no longer visit him, mâ baqiet ozêyiroh; or, mâ abqa fie mozêyiratoh.

3. For Almost, it is classical to use Cêd. Thus, They *almost* touch one another, *cédou* yetemâssou; where Cêd is rendered, "he failed narrowly."

4. Faris employs this verb with the negative for Scarcely: Lâ yecêd toujad, (the one humped camel) is *scarcely* found. But Bocthor and Catafago take no notice of Çêd. Freytag and Kazimirski give it just opposite senses, though both agree that Wala ceudan (not even scarcely) means *not at all*. The language needs a word for "scarcely;" Bil jehd, *by effort*, is not always appropriate. Whether Bocthor's word Xanien can be often used is not at all clear. In the "Algiers Mercury" I read, "Bil *ceid* Ḣatte qaÏaÏ mesêfet miel wa nuÖf," he *hardly* even traversed the distance of a mile and a half. Perhaps *bil ceud* was intended.

5. We constantly say, "He *continues* to work," for, "he is *still* working." So the Arabs have, Mâ zêl (he has not ceased = Lem yezel) with the Adverbial participle, for Still, or with the aorist. This is both popular and classical. Baîdoh for "still" (as, RaÞeit el celb, baîdoh ḣaïyan, Rob. Crusoe, I saw the dog, still alive), though popular, is hard to defend. De Perceval calls it Maronite Arabic.

6. For "he rises early," "come early to me," they may use the verb Beccir (II.), to *be early* at a thing. Kazimirski

has Beccirou, for, they were too early (at the evening prayer), which shows the verb not to be confined to the morning.

The classical language has many curious verbs that imply time; as, Rouli, go *in the evening*, Isri, travel *by night*, Obcor, do something *early*, etc.; but the sense of these is now modified.

§ 18. ANCIENT CASES OF THE NOUN.

154. The ancient Noun had three possible *Cases*, which I venture to call the Absolute, the Postpositive, and the Adverbial Cases. (To name them Nominative, Genitive, and Accusative, suggests false ideas to a Western learner.) Duals, plurals in -*oun*, and certain adjectives, had but two cases, which may be called Absolute and Oblique. We will speak of these last first.

In the Dual the Absolute is in -*án*, -*én*, the Oblique in -*ain*, -*ein*.

In the Perfect Plural, the Absolute is in -*oun*, -*öun*, the Oblique in -*ien*, -*uin*.

In the modern language the forms in -*án*, -*oun*, are almost confined to the simple predicate which has no copula expressed (see 117-120), and even there is not insisted on. The form in -*án*, -*oun*, is also used in careful style for a direct nominative (*i.e.* subject of a verb), when it is not affected by any introductory particle.

155. The three cases are marked by the inflexions -*on*, -*in*, -*en* (-*an*), when the noun is *undefined;* but these are never written in the text. Moreover, if the noun be defined the *n* falls away; leaving only -*o*, -*i*, -*e* (-*a*). It is impossible for

the modern tongue to retain these; for the final -*o* at once suggests the sense -*oh* (his), and final -*i* the sense (my), except indeed another suffix be attached, which begins with a consonant. Thus we can without inconvenience say, Bilâdo-com, Bilâdi-com, Bilâda-com. But this being limited to the suffixes -*hé*, -*com*, -*hom*, is not worth while to retain, or at least, as a fact, has not been retained. Whether it is worth while to struggle for Li bilâdi-com, as better than Li bilâd-com, or Li bilâda-com, is evidently an unsettled question with Faris and Catafago. The learner has at present a right to ignore the -*o*, -*i*, -*a*, entirely.

156. The inflexion -*on* also (it seems) is confined to poetry and ancient style. The rules of grammar concerning -*on* and -*an* are so complex and so arbitrary, that, once lost, they are of necessity irrecoverable by a nation. As they never conduce to perspicuity or any imaginable good, we have a right to rejoice that they are dead. [If they are still retained among the Wahabees, as Mr. Palgrave seems to say, that will not lead to their renewed use elsewhere.]

157. The Postpositive Case was assumed by a noun, chiefly, 1. After a preposition. 2. After an adjective, or pronoun adjective, preceding its noun. 3. After another noun with which it is in composition. In the last it is like the Latin *genitive*; in the second it is monstrously unlike. In Art. 31 it was remarked that ᴧou ῾aql, intelligent, after Fair, passes into Fair ᴧie ῾aql. Here ᴧie is the Postpositive Case of ᴧou. Such an idiom is now exceptional. The only general question in the modern dialect is, whether at all to retain -*i*, -*in*, after a preposition. To Min bilâd*i*-com, and such like, allusion has been made. In phrases which are equivalent to an adverb,

the termination -*in* is not certainly quite dead. Catafago's Dictionary (at least in the Anglo-Arabic part) may be said to represent modern *mercantile* Arabic; and he has many such phrases as the following,—the noun being undefined:

| Intentionally, bi qaˀsd*in*. | Grievously, bi colli ſamm*in*. |
| Impetuously, bi xiddat*in*. | Incautiously, bi colli ſaflat*in*. |

When two nouns following an adverb are joined by *wa*, he generally adds *in* to the former only:

Sluggishly, bi coll(i) ceselˡ*in* wa ihmâl.
Stingily, bi coll(i) ˀamaˀ*un* wa bokl. (Yet elsewhere, bi coll ˀamaˀ. Also: Intently, bi coll(i) jaddˡ*in* wa jehdˡ*in*.

When the noun is followed by an adjective, he generally adds -*in* to the noun alone. Thus:

Signally, bi wejh*in* mexhour.
In a happy hour, bi sêˀat*in* mesˀoudat.

Perhaps these are mere attempts of merchants to read Arabic like scholars. I cannot remember to have heard anything of the sort in my narrow experience; nor does C. de Perceval mention it any more than De Braine.

158. The Adverbial Case is extremely common, 1. For forming adverbs, whether from noun, adjective, or participle, as, Xaiˤen, somewhat; Baſtaten, suddenly; Baˀuidan, afar; Dâyiman, always. 2. With a noun which expresses either a point of time or duration of time; as, Gadan, on the morrow (from Gad, Gadwa, in nominative); Nehêran wa leilan, by day and by night; Xehran cêmilan, an entire month; ˀuxrien yeuman, for twenty days. 3. As said in 119, Jâ rêciban, he came riding. But we must enlarge this to contain *every indirect Predicate;* thus, I made him happy, Ana

jaTaltoh seTuid*an* (*i.e.* in a happy *state*). 4. The Cognate Accusative of our Latin and Greek grammars is rendered by the Adverbial Case; in fact, we generally need a preposition in English; as, they rejoiced *with* mighty joy: Farahou faraHa*n* Taʒuim*an*. Akin to this is the double accusative, Melli el ceˀs nebieᴧ*en*, which we must render, "Fill the glass *with* wine." Yet both these instances belong to "high style." 5. When an undefined noun is complement to an adjective (as in 14) it falls into the adverbial case, as Taʒuim qowwaten. But this is perhaps more antiquated than Taʒuim el qowwa. 6. After *Inna*, which opens a clause, nearly like "As regards," writers add the adverbial case; thus, Inna kâdim*an* fie eˀHad el adyira, now as regards a servant in one of the abbeys.

The misfortune of this adverbial case, is, that in unpointed prose even the learned neglect it with *feminines* in *at*, *et*; and do so for the highly unsatisfactory reason, that in that case, no textual "Elif" is added to guide the reader's eye! This suggests that the idiom utterly died out and has been partially recovered by learned effort. If it cannot be recovered for feminines as well as masculines it does not seem worth any pains. To limit the use strictly to adverbs seems then the wiser course.

159. It may be well here to observe that though an undefined noun or adjective in the predicate remains unmodified, if the copula verb (is, are) is understood; yet when some verb like Cên (was), Ȝuir (is become), etc., is expressed, the predicate at once falls into the adverbial case, exactly as in Jâ rêcib*an*. This seems at first unnatural; but it must be considered that Cên wezier, means, A vizier existed; *there*

was a vizier. Hence if we wish to say, *He was* a vizier, it relieves ambiguity to express it by, Cên wezier*an*. After all, we may soften the harshness of the last to ourselves, by regarding it as equivalent to, He was *for* a vizier, Erat *pro ministro regis*. The adverbial case is still used in dictionaries to express the Western accusative following an active verb, when the noun is indefinite; as, Raʿeit rajol*an*, I saw *a* man. This certainly is not popular; it belongs to a scientific notation.

PART III.—PRAXIS.

§ 1. TABLES OF PLURALS.

IIIrd type, xomous, شُمُوس ; molouc, مُلُوك. The singular is very often of the type xams, شَمْس, sometimes xetle, شَتْلَة, fem.

بَحْر	sea, boḥour (or 4, 5)	سرج	saddle, sorouj
بقل	potherb(s), boqoul	ظهر	back, λöhour
بقرة	cow (ox), boqour	نجم	star, nojoum
بطن	belly, boṭoun	نهر	river, nohour (or 4)
دمع	tear, domouʕ	زهرة	flower, zohour (or 4)
درب	road, doroub	نسر	eagle, nosour
غصن	bough, foʃöun (or 4)	قلب	heart, qoloub
حلق	throat, ḥolouq	قرن	horn, qoroun
حرش	forest, ḥoroux (or 4)	صخرة	rock, ʃökour
حقل	field, ḥoqoul	لحم	flesh, meat; loḥoum

pl. sodoud   koṭöuʕ   kodoud   soyouf   boyout
     ʔoyoun   foʕous   roʕous   ʕoʃoul   ʕomour

كؤوس دُور خيول غيوم دُور طيور جنود نقود

qidra, kettle,	pl.	قدور	qird, male ape,	pl. قرود
ḥuṣn, fortress,		حصون	jiᴅr, root (as turnip),	جذور
jild, hide, skin,		جلود	jiᴅʕ, bole, trunk,	جذوع
jisr, bridge,		جسور	ʕurq, root, vein,	عروق

IVth type, aqmâr, اقمار ; aulâd, اولاد .

ḥarx, forest, pl.	احراش	mauja, wave, pl.	امواج
kobz, bread,	اخباز	marᴅ, disease,	امراض
welad, child,	اولاد	qofl, padlock,	اقفال
maṭar, rain,	امطار	sinn, tooth,	اسنان
xajara, tree,	اشجار	ḥajar, stone,	احجار
kaxab, timber,	اخشاب	qalam, reedpen,	اقلام
marse, cord,	امراس	ḥabl, rope,	احبال
jesed, body,	اجساد	qixr, husk,	اقشار
jism, substance, (3)	اجسام	bâb, door,	ابواب
jirm, body, bulk, (3)	اخرام	rieḥ, wind,	ارياح

انهار ابحار اطراف اشيا اغصان اخبار اعدا اوقات

Vth type, rijâl, رِجَال. Common with adjectives whose singular is of the form cebier, كَبِير.

rajol, man, pl.	رجال	belad, district, pl.	بلاد
celb, dog,	كلاب	ḥajar, stone,	حجار(ة)
bafl, mule,	بغال	bint, girl,	بنات
jebal, mountain,	جبال	ḥaiṭ, wall,	حياط

baḥr, sea,	pl.	بحار	kaimar, tent,	pl.	خيام
siete, plate,		سيات	ḏieb, wolf,		ذياب
raṭab, fresh date,		رطاب	θaub, garment,		ثياب
ṣaḥfa, platter,		صحاف			
			θiyâb for θiwâb.		

cibâr, ʿuẓâm, ṣuḏâr, milâḥ, diyâr (*precincts*), nisê (*women*.)

VIᵗʰ type, ʿomarâ, أُمَرَا; ʿolemâ, عُلَمَا (learned men).

wezier, vizier,	pl.	وزرا	jêhil, ignorant,	pl.	جهلا
weciel, deputy,		وكلا	sefieh, wanton,		سفها
sefier, ambassador,		سفرا	ʿesier, captive,		اسرا

raʾies, captain, chief, pl. roʾesê.

VIIᵗʰ type, cottêb, كُتَّاب; tojjâr, تُجَّار; especially from a participial adjective formed as تاجر كاتب (Mercantile or *Reduplicate* Plural). Thus, طُلَّاب, قُطَّاع, جِهَّال, حُكَّام.

VIIIᵗʰ type, especially from singulars of the form مكان; zemân, pl. ezmina (Dactylic Plural).

mecên, place, pl.	أمكنة	χau, a light, pl.		اضوية
zemân, time,	ازمنة	lisên, tongue,		السنة
jenâḥ, wing,	اجنحة	ḥusân, horse,		احسنة
metêʿ, piece of property,	امتعة	ɣolâm, groom (lad, young man),		اغلمة
ʿamoud, pillar,	اعمدة	silâḥ, weapon,		اسلحة
libês, trowser,	البسة			

In a *surd* root transposition takes place; as, from Serier, cradle, throne, pl. Esirra, for Esrira; Hilêl, crescent moon, pl. Ehilla for Ehlila.

ixth (False Dual). 1st with three strong radicals, less common. Γolâm, lad, *pl.* Γolmân, غُلْمان; Bilâd, country, *pl.* Boldân, بُلدان; XaƮba, rod, stick, *pl.* XoƮbân, شطبان. Niswân, women. 2nd with *hollow* root; Nâr, fire, *pl.* Nierân, نيران.

Ʈaud, pole, stick, *pl.* Ʈuidân,	عيدان
sêq, leg, *pl.* sieqân,	سيقان
Ḣayiƭ, Ḣaiƭ, wall, *pl.* Ḣuiƭân,	حيطان
kaiƭ, thread, *pl.* kieƭân (3),	خيطان
xâle, a shawl, *pl.* شال or شيلان	
xâbb, young man in prime, *pl.* xobban,	
ʃabi, boy, *pl.* ʃobyân,	صبيان

xth (Short Plural), Borce, pool, *pl.* Boreç; Mediena, city, *pl.* modon.

ʿomma, nation, *pl.* omam,	امم
joθθa, carcase, *pl.* joθeθ,	جثث
dobba, bear, *pl.* dobab,	دبب
quƭƭa, cat, *pl.* quƭaƭ,	قطط
mille, sect, *pl.* milel,	ملل
qazèn, cauldron, *pl.* qozon,	قُزُن
luḣâf, counterpane, *pl.* loḣof,	
sefiena, ship, *pl.* sofon,	سُفُن

The learner may practise himself in Arabizing the nouns which here remain in European type.

§ 2. EXERCISES ON *OF*.

It was observed above that our *of* is often evaded in Arabic. In fact, we also can say, Love *to* one's country, A desire *after* riches, A hankering *for* food; which supersede *of* by another preposition. This is done especially when the former of two nouns is a *verbal* substantive, of which the Arabs also take advantage. Examples:

El modâfaʕa ʕan el selʕana, the defence of the empire.
El akbâr ʕan moqâbala, the news of a personal meeting.
Ḣusêb ʕan afʕâlihom, account of their doings.
Uḣtiyâj ila kidmathê, need of her service.
Lozoumoh min el mawâsir, his need of the water-pipes.
El temettoʕ bil hedou, the enjoyment of tranquillity.
Ana xâhid ʕala aʕmâliho, I am witness of his works.
El cefâya fil jonoud el baḣirieya, the sufficiency of the marine troops.
Bil raſm ʕan el amʕâr, in spite of the rains.
Lâ makâfa min tejdied il fetn, (there is) not fear *of* the renewal of the uproar.
ʕalb qarẋ min mablaſ darâhim, a demand of a loan *of* a sum of money.

> Oqqat ʕasel, an ounce of honey.
> Milʕaqat maʕdan, a spoon of metal.
> Cies min el ḣarier, a pouch of silk.
> ˀSoḧöun bellaur, dishes of fine glass.
> Uḣda' tile el aʕdâd, one of those numbers.
> Ceθier min afˀsâniho, many of its boughs.

Ana moxakkuꭍ li meliecetí, I am a representative of my queen.
Arbaᵀ̃ mieya beit min xiᵀ̃ri, four hundred stanzas of my poetry.
Hie ᵀ̃ala aHsen Hâl min el râHa, it is in the best state of repose.
Dimaxq cênet maHaᵀ̃ᵀ̃ lil uΔᵀ̃urâb, Damascus was a focus of commotion.
Fa⁵emma ꭍârat el⁵ân menzilan liḷ selâm, wa mercezen lil hedou, yet it has become now an abode of peace, and a centre of tranquillity.
Jebal Lobnân hou manbaᵀ̃ liḷ xiqâq wa el fetn, Mount Lebanon is a fountain of division and sedition.
El sêᵀ̃a ᵀ̃axara min eḷ nehêr, the hour ten of the day.
Rajfa qawieya min zelzelet il ⁵erΔ, a strong shock of earthquake.
Eḷ ꭍâyiH jemieᵀ̃oh min el akxâb, the quarter (is) all of it of wood (timbers).
Fie mecênain min jism el imrâa, in two places of the woman's body.
El qoᵀ̃b eḷ ximâlieya min el cor⁵et el ⁵erΔuiya, the north pole of the terrestrial globe.
Cên wâbil maᵀ̃ar ⁵ems, there was a heavy shower of rain yesterday.
Jomhour wâfir min aᵀ̃yân el ⁵ehêli, an abundant concourse of the chief men of the population.
Ziyâdat fâyidat eḷ ꭍolH, the immensity of the advantage of peace.
Sorᵀ̃at quꭍâꭍ jinâyatoh, the swiftness of the punishment of his offence.
Min ᵀaraf jelâlet Imperâᵀ̃öur Numsê, on the part of the majesty of the Emperor of Austria.

§ 3. SMALL TALK, WITHOUT VERBS.

Min ein baflac heʌêc ? whence is that mule of thine ?
Houa min Ispânia, he is from Spain.
Bafli aḤsen min Ḥumârec, my mule is better than thy ass.
Wa Ḥuʃâni aḤsen min baflec, and my horse is better than thy mule.
Ḥuʃânoh cediex faqaϓ, his horse is a gelding (hack) only.
Liḷ darb el cediex kair, for the road *a* hackney is good.
Ϯala 'ḷ darb leis melieḤ el ceḤail, on the road *a* bloodhorse is not good.
El bafl melieḤ liḷ sefar, *a* mule is good for travel.
El ʿerX ϓaiyiba honâ jiddan, the soil is very good here.
ʿErX Ḥaleb collohe mokʃuba, the soil of Aleppo is all fertile.
Hie jaiyida, maϒloum ! it is excellent, no doubt!
Collohe sehile wa wâsiϒa honâ, all of it is level and wide here.
Honâ monêsiba liḷ rocoub, here it is suited for riding.
Walêcin honêlic waϒura jiddan, yet yonder it is very rugged.
Ei naϒam : el jibâl ϒâliya, yes ; the mountains are high.
Fiḷ doroub ϓuin ceθier, in the roads is plentiful clay (mud).
El jémal leis monêsib liḷ ϓuin, the camel is not suited to mud.
MelieḤ el bafl ϒala'l jébal, the mule is good on the mountain.
Fiḷ sehl aḤsen el jémal, on the plain, better is the camel.
El jemal qawi wa mêcin, the camel is strong and stout,
Walêcin ajra' el Ḥuʃân, yet swifter (is) the horse.
Maϒloum : akfaf el kail, no doubt ! horses are lighter.
El bifâl fie bilâdi melieḤa, the mules in my country are good.
Bifâlecom aϓwal min bifâlina, your mules are taller than ours.
Naϒam ; ccbar wa aqwa', yes ; bigger and stronger.

Robbama el ḥumâr ᶜandacom cebier, possibly the ass with you is large.

Fie bilâdina el ḥamier ᶜaſiera, in our country the asses are small.

Bil ḥaqq! leisou ḥamier, bel jiḥâx, in truth! they are not asses, but donkeys.

El jaḥx ᶜanied, motᶜub jiddan, the donkey is stubborn, very tiresome.

Ꞩaᶜb lil rocoub, wa bâṭu, difficult for riding, and slow.

El biſâl ᶜandana ſâliya, the mules with us are dear.

El baſl aſla' min el cediex, the mule is dearer than the hackney,

Bel min el ḥuꞨân aiᴅan, nay, even than the horse too.

Lâ! el ceḥail el ᶜeꞨliey aſla' bil ceθier, no! the genuine bloodhorse is dearer by far.

Ein ibnec el najjâr? where is thy son the carpenter?

Hou ſâyib ᶜanna min xehrain, he is absent from us for two months.

Hêᴅih el sêᶜa houa fie Baſdâd, (at) this hour (moment) he is in Bagdad.

Hel zeujetoh maᶜoh honêc? is his wife with him there?

Lâ: bel collo ᶜailetoh honâ, no, but all his family is here.

E tile el bilâd aḥsen min bilâdina? is that country better than our country.

Ḥâlethe melieḥa, bil ḥaqq, its condition is good, in truth.

Leiset aḥsen min ḥâletna fie colli xaiᶜ, it is not better than our state in everything.

Coll el matjar honêlic auseᶜ minnoh ᶜandana, all the trade yonder (is) wider than it (is) with us.

Tile el bilâd ḥârra ceθieran, that country is hot excessively.

El xams aḥarr minnehe honâ, the sun is hotter than she is here.

El belda mel'âna min el ſabar, the town is full of dust.

Ṭand el enhêr eḷ rief moθmir, along the rivers the country is fruitful.

Eḷ donyâ sokina fiḷ Ṯaif, the world is hot in the summer.

El Ḫoqoul qâḫula min el Ḫarr, the fields are parched by the heat.

§ 4. AT THE CLOSE OF A JOURNEY.

Eḷ donyâ moſayyima, the world (sky) is cloudy.

Θârat eḷ rieḪ, the wind has sprung up.

TemṮor, Ṯala ẓanni, fiḷ sêṮa, it will rain, in my opinion, in a minute.

WâqiṮ maṮar fil boṮda, rain (is) falling in the distance.

Wa iᴀe! jâyi Ṯalaina, and lo! (it is) coming on us.

ṮaḪuiḪ! el maṮar zekâk (ſazier), true! the rain is profuse (copious).

El Ḫamd lillâh! mâ hou ṮaqieṮ, thank God! it is not sleet.

Θiyâbi mabloula, my clothes are wetted.

Leeinni lest bardân ceθieran, yet I am not extremely cold.

Hêᴀe el maṮar hou dâfi, this rain is warm.

Nadfa' (Netedaffa') baṮdoh (baṮdan), we shall get warm afterwards.

Hel el kân baṮuid min honâ? is the caravansery far hence?

El mesêfe moqârib mielein, the distance is about two miles.

El waḪal Ṯamieq jiddan, the mire is deep, very.

MaṮloum! cên wâbilan min maṮar, surely! it was a torrent of rain.

El'ên wâqiṮa raxxa faqaṮ, now (is) falling a drizzle only.

E baſlec teṮbân min eḷ Ṯuin, is thy mule wearied by the mud?

Baſli mâ hou θêbit jiddan, my mule is not firm, very.
Cetifoh semiece ceθieran, his shoulder is too thick.
Qawâyimoh raqieqa bil ſâya, his legs are delicate in extreme.
Dâbba miθl hêᴀe arda' min ḫumâr, a beast like this is worse than an ass.
Walêcin ᴋahroh ʕarieᴋ, yet his back is broad.
Hêhona ʒârat el ˤerᴋ yêbise, here the ground is become dry.
El darb auseʕ minnohe qablan, the road is wider than it (was) before.
ʕaiyib! el dawâbb naxieʕa (nixâʕ), good! the beasts are in spirits.
Ehêh! naʒul ila'l kân fil sêʕa, ha! we shall reach the caravansery quickly.
Qoddâmana nês ceθieroun, before us are many people.
Collohom rêciboun, all of them riding.
Leisou jemieʕhom rijâl, they are not all men.
Honêlic niswân min baʕuid, yonder are women afar.
El niswân ecθar min el rijâl, . . . (are) more numerous than. . .
ʕala ʒanni, hie qâfila, in my opinion it is a caravan (company of travellers).
ᴀêlic hejien abyaᴋ, that yonder is a white dromedary.
Min jomlathom jiḫâx ceθiera, among them are many donkeys.
Wa honêc rajolein ʕala jemal, and there, two men on a camel.
Selâm ʕalaicom, peace (be) to you.
Wa ʕalaicom el selâm, and to you (be) peace.
Baláſna ila 'l menzil, we have reached the alighting place.
Hel menʒöum el kân? is the caravansery well arranged.
Oʒbór daqieqa; fa naʕrif, be patient a moment, then we (shall) know.

§ 5. AT THE CARAVANSERAI.

Cennis auɣati, sweep my chamber.
Leis xai⁵ honâ menʒöum, not (any) thing here is well arranged.
Cennest el ⁵erɣuiya, yâ kawâja, I have swept the floor, sir.
El micnese menʒouꞇa, the broom (is) spoiled.
Firâxi leis naɣuif, my bed is not clean.
Ente naꞇsên, yâ âki (âkoui)! thou art sleepy, O my brother.
Lâ taꞇfi el̤ nâr, do not put out the fire.
El̤ nâr (*fem.*) inꞇafat, is put out.
Bi weddina ſadâ⁵, we want dinner.
Oqꞇod ꞇala'l̤ diewân, sit on the sofa.
Ijlis janbi, sit by me.
Ijlis ꞇand el̤ sofra, sit at the table (tray of leather).
Jieb el ſadâ⁵, bring the dinner.
Ḧöꞇꞇ el̤ ꞇaꞇâm ꞇala'l̤ sofra, put down the food on the table.
Nâwilni sicciena, hand me a knife.
Onâwiloh lec, hêhonâ, I hand it to thee,—here.
Etenâwiloh min yedac, I receive it from thy hand.
Hel oqaddim lec laḧme? shall I present a bit of meat?
Lâzimni soteiya (sicte: *Alep.*), I need (opus mihi) a plate.
Ein el̤ siyât (*Alep.*)? where are the plates?
A ꞇandac el̤ ꙅöḧöun? are the dishes with you?
Collohe maꞇ el̤ secêcien, all of them with the knives.
Collohe cênet fie korji, all of them were in my saddle bags.
Hêhona el̤ ꙅöḧoun Ḧâɣura, here (are) the dishes ready.
Coll xai⁵ qoddâmacom, everything (is) before you.
'Koᴀ laḧme maꞇ cisrat kobz, take morsel of bread.
'Col min el̤ rozz maꞇan, eat (some) of the rice together.

Oried semne maᵀ el kobz, I wish a (piece of) butter with the bread.

ᵀase toried el milḤ, perhaps you wish the salt.

Mâ cᶜol ceθier min el milḤ, I do not eat much of salt.

Aᵀyab el zobd min el semn ᵀandi, nicer is fresh butter than salt butter in my opinion.

Min kâᵀuri aḤsen el jobon, from my liking better (is) cheese.

Lécin mâ texrab xaiᶜ, but you do not drink (any) thing.

Cênet el jarra melᶜâna, the urn was full.

RouḤ! jieb el bellaura, go! bring the decanter.

Fiehe limonâda ᵀaiyibe, in it (is) nice lemonade.

Lâ kloᵀ fiehi mây, do not mix in it water.

Leiset Ḥölwa ceθieran, it is not sweet too much.

Xarâb el borteqân yoᵀjibni aḤsen, orange-wine (sherbet) pleases me better.

Melli qadaḤui, fill my goblet.

Ceᶜs ᵌaſiera tecfieni ana, a small glass suffices *me*.

E ᵀoried teᶜcol ezyad (zed, *Alg.*—cemân, *Syria*), wishest thou to eat more?

Aᵀᵀᵤini xiqqat el ᶜokra', give me the other piece (half).

Bi weddi cᶜol xoqfa cemân (*Alep.*), I will eat a slice more.

Kalliʃ hêᴧih el cisra, finish this morsel.

Héhona loqma ᵀaiyibe, here is a nice mouthful.

Esteθir bi kairac, I wish multiplication to your welfare (*i.e.* I thank you).

Ceθθer kairac! (God) multiply thy welfare!

Kalaᵌna: xiel el ᵌöḤöun, we have done: remove the dishes.

Hel toried texrab* *toton* (*Alep.*)? wishest thou to smoke tobacco?

* *Drink*.

Ṭan ʼiᴧnec, ana mâ axrab, by thy leave, I smoke not.
Mâ aḥöbb qalioun, I do not love a straight pipe (*Alep.*).
El̤ narjiele taqṬaṬ ṭaqli aḥsen; lau cên kâṬuri, en axrab,
  The cocoanut* hits my mind better; if it were my liking that
    I smoke.
El iθnain farad xaiˢ ṭandi, the two (are but) one thing with me.
Robbama teḥobb qahwe au txây? possibly thou lovest coffee
  or tea?
Lâ: oried el̤ râḥa, I wish rest.
Melieḥ! ente testerieḥ, good! *thou* shall take rest.
Naḥna naxrab el̤ txây? *we* will drink tea.
Hel el mây sokn? is the water hot?
AṬṬuini mowaiya sokna, give me a little water hot.
Adier bâlec, yaʿli el mây, turn thy mind (that) the water boil.
Hêᴧe el finjân ʽSaʿier, this coffee-cup (is too) small.
Jieb Ṭâse: hiya ecbar, bring a cup (flat cup) (saucer): this
  is bigger.
ḤoṬṬ txây bil cefâya, put in tea in sufficiency.
Iṭmeloh qawi, make it strong.
Mâ axrab txây min ʿair ḥalieb, I do not drink tea without
  milk.
Kairieya, enna ṭandana ḥalieb, (it is) good luck that we have
  milk.
Bel honâ qaimâq aiẋan, nay, here is clotted cream too.
Ġair enna leis maṭui soccer Ingliez, only that I have not with
    me English sugar.
Ṭase taqdir texraboh bila soccer? perhaps thou art able to
    drink it without sugar?

---

* Alep.—*i.e.* The pipe in which the smoke passes through water in a cocoanut shell.

Aradt exteri min soccer, fa min qillet bakt, mâ
I wished (that) I buy some sugar, then, by ill luck, did not
  baqiyat wala oqqa wâḧuda, Ṭand eḷ doccên.
  remain not even a single ounce at the shop.
Mâ yaẊörr, it does not hurt.
Mâ lâzim eḷ soccer, not needful (is) sugar.
Melli eḷ Ṭâse, fill the cup.
TefaẊẊal, wa ixrab, do favour, and drink.
Axcor faẊlec wa jamielec, I thank thy favour and thy politeness.
Bila Ḧalieb Ṭari au qaxta, mâ yaȝuḧḧ eḷ txây,
Without fresh milk or cream, is not right the tea.
Lau cont Ṭalabt qahwe minni, toujad Ṭandi qahwe
If thou hadst demanded coffee of me, is found with me coffee
  min Mauka, el qahwet el Ḧamrâ,
  of Moka, the coffee the red.
Toxarrifni: lêcin aḧabb liya eḷ txây,
Thou honourest me; but more acceptable to me (is) tea.
Ṭala kâṬurae, according to thy pleasure.
E toried eḷ Ṭâset el ⁺okra'? dost wish a second cup.
Lâ: wâḧuda teefieni (toceffieni), no: one suffices me.
Yaȝuḧḧ, all is right.

§ 6. ON DESSERT.

Hel Ṭandac xai⁺ liḷ noql (*dessert*)?
Ṭandi anwâṬ xette' min el fawâcih,
I have kinds diverse of   fruits.

Qoul, eix' min fawâcih Ḧâᴅir ᴀel waqt,
Say, what sort of fruits (is) ready this moment.

Hehonâ zebieb, wa belaḤ, wa leuz, wa tien, wa jeuz,
Here   raisins,   dates,   almonds,   figs,   walnuts,

wa temarhindi, wa fairohe.
tamarinds, and others than these.

El zebieb ʾecl Ṭaiyib,   aḤsen min el Ƭunab Ƭandi.
Raisins (are) good eating, better than grapes (in my opinion).

Emma Ƭandi Ƭunab aiẊan melieḤa.
But with me grapes too (are) good.

Min ein texteri el   Ƭunab?
Whence buyest thou grapes?

Lâ (Mâ) axteri qaƮ; collohe min jonaineti.
I buy not at all; all of them (are) from my little garden.

Ƭase   texteri el temarhindi wa el belaḤ.
Perhaps thou buyest the tamarinds and dates.

Ḥaqq fie yedec; jonaineti   jaiyida,
(Thou art right) my garden (is) excellent,

Walêcin mâ yomcin en toḤsin coll   el fawâcih
But it is not possible that should succeed all fruits

fie mecên wâḤud.
in one place.

LaƬall tokrij   kamr min el Ƭunab.
Haply thou elicitest wine from the grapes.

Lâ; neʾcol el Ƭunab, waʾ illa noqaddidhe li zebieb.
No; we eat the grapes, or else we dry them for raisins.

Jieb liy xowaiyat el zebieb.
Give me a little   raisins.

E ʇoried te'eol kobze maʈhe?
Wilt   eat   bread with it?

Oried; fa axrab mowaiya baʈdoh.
I will, and drink water after it.

Lâ! bi faδlec!   ente lest   Moslim.
No! by thy favour! thou art not Mussulman.

El Naʒâri   leisou ʈayifien el kamr.
Christians are not abhorrers of wine.

ʒaĥuiĥ: fa   minhom   siccieroun.
True: then (some) of them are drunkards.

Min el fawâcih el ĥölwa taqdir teʈmal el dibs: fa hou ce
From sweet fruits thou canst make syrup (treacle): and it is

miθli el ʈasel.   Min el kobz wa el zebieb teʈmal
like   honey.   From bread and raisins thou makest

faʈöur melieĥ.   El kamr, wa ceʌê el nebieʌ, leis monêsib
breakfast good. Wine, and so too the toddy, is not suitable

lil faʈöur.   Wa maʈ hêʌc, el Fransêwieya fa
for breakfast.   For all that, the French

yaxrabounoh bil faʈöur   fâliban.
drink it   at breakfast prevalently.

Lâ towâkiʌni: celâmec leis maδbouʈ: lecinnehom
Reprove me not: thy speech is not accurate: but they

  yaxraboun el qahwe (*coffee*) fâliban.

Ah! ñe fair emcina   tetefayyar el ʈâda.
    different places is different the custom.

9

In tefayyar Ṭaqs el donya, fa Ḥâlan tetefayyar el maᶻêcil.
If vary the   climate, then instantly the victuals vary.

Fil Ḥarr yoᴛjibni el Ḥalieb el Ḥâmiz, wa fil bard el qahwe
In heat pleases me milk   acid,   in cold

bi Ḥalieb sokn. Ṭaiyib honâ Ḥalieb el maᴛz ; emma
with milk hot.   Nice here (is) milk of goats ; but

aṬyab ᴛandi   Ḥalieb el baqar.
nicer with me (is) milk of cows.

Δoqt ana marra(ten) Ḥalieb el jâmous, wa fie   kâṬuri hou
I tasted once   milk of buffalo, and in my liking it is

elΔeΔ min cileihoma. Li coll waḤud Δauqoh el makꝪouꝪ.
nicer than both.   To each one (is) his peculiar taste.

§ 7. TALK WITH A COOK ON CATERING.

A. Yâ Wanéss, lâzim-ni eiyâc.   W. Yâ kawâja ! eix' textehi ?
   John ! I want thee.   Sir ! what dost thou wish ?

A. Oried, en teji maᴛui ila'l souq.
   I will, that thou come with me to the market.

W. Bi weddac xaiᶻ ᴛase lil ſadâ.
   Thou wantest something perhaps for dinner.

A. Naᴛam : en texteri laḤm ſanam.
   Yes : that thou buy flesh (of) sheep.

W. Lâ, seiyidi ; mâ yaꝪuḤḤ lec.
   No, sir ! (my lord !) it will not be well for thee.

A. Fa leix' hê∆e mâ yaʒuḥḥ liya?
Then why will this not be well for me?

W. Laḥm karouf aḥsen : houa rakʒ.
Flesh of lamb is better : it is tender.

A. Lâzimni ai∆an lift wa jazer.
I need also turnips and carrots.

Ṭase fil souq ki∆âr wa boqoul.
Perhaps in the market (are) greens and potherbs.

W. Fie hê∆e elᶜên coll el ko∆âra fâliya.   A. Mâ ya∆orr.
In the present season all greens are dear.   It hurts not.

Ecθar mă yaʒuir,   el baṬn yeᶜko∆ qaliel.
Utmost that it may be, the belly takes (but) little.

W. Ṭala ʒanni, naḥna   Ṭâyizien ila jobon.
my notion, we (are) needing   cheese.

A. Hel youjad jobon fil souq ? (*is found?*)

W. Youjad honêe Ṭaiyib, rakieʒ (*cheap*).

A. Ente falṬân :   colloma hou Ṭaiyib, ʒâr fâli.
Thou (art) mistaken : whatever is good, is dear.

Hel Ṭandana xowaiya minnoh ?
Is   with us a little   of it ?

W. Mâ yabqi xaiᶜ, illa qaliel.
Nothing remains, except little.

Lâzimni semn min xân (liᶜejl) pilau.
I need butter for (*Alep.*) a rice-dish.

A. E toriedoh min xânee ente ?
Wishest thou it on account of thyself ?

W. Lâ, seiyidi : teᵀrif, fie hêᴀe el faꞋl qouti
No, my lord! thou knowest, in this season my food

el rozz bi Ḣalieb faqaᵀ.
(is) rice with milk only.

A. Faᶜemma el rozz bi semn aiᴧan hou ᵀaix (*victual*) melieḢ.

W. Ꞌadaqt. Lêcin, waᶻin ᵀaᵀâmi leis xaiᶻ leᴀieᴀ jiddan,
Thou art right. But even if my diet is not very nice,

fa melieḢ li qowweti wa moꞋuḢḢ.
yet (it is) good for my strength wholesome.

Waᶻemma cên celâmona fie laḢm lil sofratec.
But our talk was on (concerning). . . . thy table (tray).

Yomein teḢobb yaknie?
It is possible you like a stew (ragout)?

E lâ toried aᵀboq xouraba?
Dost thou not choose, I cook soup?

A. Lâ toᵀᵀuini meslouq; bel el mexwiey
Do not give me boiled (meat); nay, but roasted

aḢsen ᵀandi.
(is) better with me.

W. ꞋaḢuiḢ, lâzimec kârouf. El ᴧân mâ yecoun
Certainly, thou needest lamb. The mutton will not be

ᵀaiyib, laulâ tesloqoh. Wa ente, leix' toried teji
nice, unless thou stew it. But why wilt thou come

maᵀui? AḢsen, en exteri ana bifairee.
with me? (It is) better, that I buy without thee.

A. Ente waḥidee? Hel ẗandee folous?
   Thou alone? Hast thou money?

W. Aṫṫuini xai᷊ min   folous : fa aḥoṫṫ
   Give me somewhat of money : then I will set down

   ẗala waraqa,   eix'ma (eiyoma) exteri.
   on a paper,   whatever I buy.

A. Yaṡuḥḥ.   'Koᴀ el noqoud.
   It will do.   Take the cash.

§ 8. WITH MULETEERS ON A JOURNEY.

A. Heyâ, Heyâ! qad ṫalaẗat eḷ xams.
   Ho! Ho! already the sun has come out (up).

   Ya baffâlien, ḥammilou eḷ dawâb(b).
   O muleteers, load (II.) the beasts.

   Eḷ nehêr ṫalaẗ ẗalaina.   Qoumou!   Li nerouḤ!
   The day has risen upon us.   Get up!   Let us go!

   Yâ el cesêle'!   Leis licom xajâẗa en teqoumou?
   O ye lazy ones!   Have ye not bravery to get up?

   Teẗâl, Yousef! li noḥammil   ana wa ent.
   Come, Joseph! let us load (the mules), I and you.

B. Iᴀe cén toried, ana oḥammil wa ente temsie eḷ dâbbe;
   If thou choose, I (will) load and thou hold the beast;

   waʿilla, ana amsiche, wa ente toḥammil.
   or else, I will hold her, and thou shalt load.

A. Lâ lâ! aḥsen en arboʈhe   fil   ʿibziem;   θomm inna
   No!   better that I fasten her in the buckle;   thereupon

   noḥammil iθnaina sewâ sewâ.
   we (shall) load, we two together.

   El aḥmâl θaqiele, wala yaqdir wâḥud waḥdoh ʈala' ʿen
   The loads are heavy, nor is able one (man) alone for that

   yarfaʈhe.   Ḥammil ente min jânib, wa ʿana oḥammil
   he lift them. Load thou from (one) side, and I (will) load

   min el jânib el ʿokra'.   Fehemt xaiʿ minni?
   from the other side (f). Hast thou at all understood me?

B. Melieḥ! li narfaʈ ʈala'l baʿala.—Yecfi.
   Good!   let us lift upon the mule.—It suffices.

A. Lâ! irfaʈ   ezyad.
   No! lift (it) more.

B. ᐃel waqt eḷ   rafâʈa   biḷ ziyâda.
   This time the lifting (is) in excess.

A. Waʈʈu,   Ḥatte' yecoun colloh sewa'.
   Lower (it), until it shall be all of it even.

B. Orboʈ min jânibec, wa aʈʈuini el ḥabl.
   Tie   from thy side, give me the rope.

A. Melieḥ hêceᐃê.   B. 'Koᐃoh!
   Good in that way.   Take it!

A. Oʃbor xowaiya! Héᐃe   qaʃuir. Mâ   yecfi.
   Wait a bit.   This (is) (too) short. It does not suffice.

   Ḥöll   elleᐃi rabaʈtoh,   wa ʈawwiloh.
   Loosen (that) which thou hast tied, and lengthen it.

B. Melieḧ! Nàwílni   el Ṭaraf. Imsic!
   Good! Hand (III.) to me the end. Hold (it)!

A. Ana mêsicoh.   Fil sêṭa   Ḧammil!
   I (am) holding it. Now (this moment) load!

B. Ana moḦammil. Yâ, eix' hêᴀe el mirbaṬa?
   I (am) loading. O, what (is) this fastening?

   Mâ ana qâdir aḧöll he. (Lest ana qâdir ṭala ḧallihe.)
   I am not able to untie it.

A. IqṬaṬhe bi   mousi.
   Cut it with my clasp knife.

B. Lâlâ: yecoun kisêra: fa baṬdoh   mâ
   No: it would be a loss (a pity); then afterwards it is

   yeswa' xai².   Aḧsen   el Ṣabr.
   worth nothing. Patience is better.

   Wa Ḧallaitoh [ḧalaltoh]. 'Koᴀ el Ḧabl, wa xouf [onʒor]
   And I have untied it.   Take the rope, and see (look)

   imma hêᴀe yecfiec.   A. Yecfi. Orboṭ melieḧ,
   whether this suffices thee.   Tie it well

   wa irmi liya   Ṭaraf el Ḧabl min teḧt baṬn il dâbba.
   throw to me the end of the rope under belly of the beast.

B. Ḧêᴀe hou el Ṭaraf. Imsícoh.   A. Ana mêsicoh.
   This is the end.   Hold it.   I am holding it.

   Xoddoh   ecθar min jihtee. B. Yaʒuḧḧ.   Ireéb!
   Tighten it more thy side.   All is right. Mount!*

---

* The verb means either Mount or Ride; so, either Get on board a ship, or, Make a voyage.

C. Kallicni amxi xowaiya, wa el bafla terouĦ qoddâm.
   Let me walk a bit,   shall go in front.

B. Lâ! hêᴅih   dâbbe, leis   minhe   xaiᶻ   melieĦ:
   (as for) this animal, there is nothing good from her:

   terfis   wa tercoᴧ; wa iᴅe herabat,   mâ   yomcin
   she kicks and runs;   if she has fled, not is possible

   ilĦâqohê.   Lâzimec,   imma   terceb,   au
   overtaking her.   You must   either   ride,   or

   temsiche   dâyiman bil lijâm. El iktiyâr   ᶜaleic.
   you hold her always by the bridle. The choice (is) on thee.

   ᶜala   kâᶜurec.
   According to thy liking.

C. Cên liya   teᶜab ceθier: el rocoub   aĦsen.
   Was to me fatigue much: riding (is) better.

   Sêᶜudni min faᴧlec.   B. B'ism Illâh! ircéb!
   Assist me by thy favour.

D. ᶜa ana,   bi weddi areeb waĦdi.
   As for me, (it is) in my wish to mount alone.

   Imsic el dâbbe, liᶻella tehrib minni.
   Hold the beast, lest she flee from me.

B. Ircebt* melieĦ: ente   xâᶜur.
   Thou hast mounted well: thou (art) clever.

D. Hel ana mâ qoltoh lec?   B. Miel xowaiya ᶜala kalf,
   Did I not tell thee?   Lean a little backward,

---

* To mount without stirrups on to a travelling saddle is very difficult.

Ḣatte'   terceb aḢsen.   Souq ila qoddâm.
that thou mayest ride   better.   Drive forward.

Ana mosêƔud el ˤekâra', wa   arja Ɣileie baƔdoh.
I (am) helping the others,   I return to thee afterwards.

RouḢ xowaiya   xowaiya, Ɣala sohouletec.   A. RouḢ bil
Go   (rowaidan) gently, at thy ease.   in

Ɣajl: xouc, xouc!   B. Collohom   Ḣammalou, wa
haste! prick!   All of them have laden, and (are)

hom jâyien warâna.   C. Ente teƔabt   ceθiera.
coming behind us.   art tired (hast toiled) too much.

B. Ah! mâ hou xai˨ hêᴀe el xiqâ.   Hêᴀih hie ꜤanâƔatna.
   is nothing this misery (toil).   This is our trade (*art*).

A. El teƔab leis fie hêᴀih, lêcin fil molâqâyat il Ɣarab,
   The fatigue is not in this, but in the meeting of the Arabs,

   elleᴀien auqât auqât yoƔarriyounna ; wa baƔƛ   el
   who   times times strip us (naked) ;   a part of the

   kofarâ   yozallimou Ɣalaina : hêᴀe hou el teƔab elleᴀi
   road-guards oppress us   which

   naḢn lesna   moteƔawwidien Ɣalaihi.
   we are not accustomed   to.

Waˤemma, ˤemr el teḢmiel wa el ḢaƔƔ fa hou sehil Ɣalaina.
But the affair of loading and depositing is easy to us.

C. El hewa Ɣaiyib elyeum.   B. Ɣaiyib, el Ḣamd lillâh!
   The air is nice to-day.   praise to God!

A. NaƔmel   el-yeum θelâθien miel.
   We make to-day 30   miles.

D. Wa ceif bi weddicom tercebou Ṭöul eḷ nehêr?
how will you ride all the day?

A. Lâ! qabl eḷ Χöhr neḧöṬṬ, ḧatte' neteʕaxxa wa
before noon we set down, until we sup and

noṬṬum eḷ dawâbb, wa baʕdoh nosêfir min jadied,
feed the beasts, afterwards we travel anew,

wala neḧöṬṬ illa qarieb min el leil.
nor set down except near (to) the night.

D. El yeum baṬaina: mâ ḧammalna illa
To-day we have been sluggish: we did not load except

baʕd Ṭolouʕ il fajr,
after coming forth of the dawn.

C. Lâ! eḷ nehêr mâ cên Ṭalaʕ liḷ sêʕa.
the day had not come forth yet.

A. Eḷ Χau, elleʌi qad raˤeitoh, cên Χau el qamar
The light which already you perceived, moon

ˤemma el fajr Ṭalaʕ, baʕdama conna ḧammalna zemân.
came forth, after that we had loaded (a long) time.

C. Ṣadaqt. Lêcin ei hie sêʕat eḷ nehêr fie ʌel waqt?
You are right. But what is the hour at this time?

A. Bil ḧaqq, yabqa ezyad (zod) ila'ḷ Χohr sêʕatein θelâθe.
In truth remains (encore) to noon two hours (or) three.

C. Lau cên sêʕa wâḧuda, lecên aḧsen el ḧöloul honâ;
If it were one hour, verily were better unpacking here,

iʌecên hêʌe el mauΧuʕ melieḧ jiddan, wa fich eḷ ʒull
since this place in it shade

wa el mây, wa el Ḥaṭab wa Ḥaxiex lil bahêyim.
water, firewood, grass for the animals.

A. Mâ yohimm: baʕdoh nolâqi fair mecên aḤsen
It imports not: afterwards we meet another place better

minnoh. Xoucou, li najri fie hêᴅe el bard.
Prick ye! let us run in this cold.

Baʕd el Ḍöhr textidd el sokouna. Fie waqtihi
After noon the heat grows intense. Instantly

nofettix lina maḤall, nestiʒull wa
we search out for us a place, in which we shade and rest

nartêḤ (VIII.) fiehi sêʕa sêʕatein.
ourselves an hour (or) two hours.

C. Maʕqoul. ʕalaic el Ḥöcm.
A wise thing. On thee (rests) the decision.

A. Hêhou el mauḍuʕ elleᴅi qolt lec ʕalaihi.
Here is (maṭraḤ) which I told thee of.

AḤsen min el auwal bi ceθier.
(It is) better than the first by much.

Ana ʕârif hêᴅe el ʕarieq melieḤ.
I know this way well.

Cem marra maxait fie hêᴅih el ʕaḤâri!
How many times (roḤt wa jiet) in these plains (desarts).

Lau cên ḤaṬṬait bâli ʕala 'l Ḥujâr,
If I had (ḤaṬaṬt) set my mind upon the stones,

le cont aʕrif coll wâḥiud bi ʕouratoh.
verily I should know each one by its figure.

140   HANDBOOK OF MODERN ARABIC.

C. Ain naḣöṪṪ?   (Ain   nenzil?) A. Inzil honâ,
   Where sit we down? (Where alight we?)   Alight here,

   teḣit hê∆ih el̦ xajara. Hie moʒallala, wa el̦ raml nâʕum.
   under this   tree.   It is shady, and the sand soft.

C. Waᶻamma honâ min ein neᶻko∆ el ḣaṪab lil maṪbak?
   But here whence take we firewood for cookery?

A. Yâ ente! hel taṪlob lec fil̦ ʃaḣrâ coll xaiᶻ
   O thou! dost thou require in the desart

   ma∆bouṪ? el̦ Ṫabâka besieṪa hona, bila   wajâq.
   accurate? the cooking is simple here, without a stove.

   Iʕmel θoqba (joura) fil̦   raml, waᶻilla 'ko∆ lec
   Make a hole   in the sand, or else take for thee

   ḣajarain   θelâθe, wa reccib Ṫalaihe el̦ Ṫanjara,
   two stones (or) three and mount on them the stewpot,

   wa axʕul teḣtehe min   baʕar il jimâl il yâbis
   and kindle beneath it (some) dung of camels dry,

   elle∆i texeufoḣ   qoddâmec, wa fil̦ sêʕa yestewi
   which (tenʒoroh) thou seest ... instantly will be dressed

   el̦ Ṫabiek, eiyoma yecoun morâdec   taṪbok.
   the dish, whatever it may be thy will (that) thou cook.

B. Ṫase toried el̦ rozz?   Hê∆e sêhil. C. Einaʕam.
   Perhaps thou wishest rice? This is easy. Yes.

   Lâ tebṪui. D. El eᶻkarien mâ yaṪbokou   xaiᶻ'.
   Be not slow.   The others do not cook (any) thing.

B. Ah! màn yeᶻcol jobon, wa màn yêᶻcol buʃâl.
      one eats cheese, another eats onions.

A. Hêhou el mây faliyân.   C. Hoțț el rozz fil may.
   Lo! the water is boiling.   Put the rice   water.

   Naḧḧu el ſitâya.   B. Leix' testeîjil hêceʌê?
   Set aside the cover.   Why hastest thou so?

C. Morâdi   arqod   qalielan, li⁵enna mâ nimt
   My wish (is that) I sleep a little, because I slept

   xai⁵   hêʌih el leile.
   not at all this   night.

B. Xouf! collohom   qadd   ⁵ecelou, wa hêʌe el sêîa hom
   See! all of them already have eaten, and at present they

   râqidien.   Fie waqtihom yaqoumou wa yoḧammilou.
   (are) sleeping.   Presently they will rise and load.

C. Ente e fa mâ te⁵eol ezyad   xai⁵ ?
   Dost not thou then eat something more?

B. Yeefi :   axcor   faᴧlec.
   It suffices : I thank thy favour.

C. Ana rayiḧ aſsil yedaiya ;   baîdoh   arqod honâ.
   I am going to wash my two hands ; afterwards I sleep here.

B. Țandama ente   râfid,   fa ana afsil el Țanjara wa el
   While thou (art) sleeping,   I wash the stewpot and the

   ȝoḧöun, fa   aḧöțțhe   fil   Țaiba.
   dishes,   then I put them into the wallet.

C. Maîloum, hêʌe el mecên Țaiyib.
   Surely,   this place is good.

   Xomm el hewâ wa el rieḧ el léti tehobb îalaina.
   Smell the air and the wind which blows upon us.

§ 9. COPTIC FEAST.

M. Xouf, yâ Fanous, imma Ḫaᴣir lina el ſadâ.
   See   Stephanus   whether ready   dinner.

F. Coll xaiˤ Ḫaᴣur.

M. Ifrax eḷ sofra wa mandielehê, wa jieb eḷ ᵀaᵀâm.
   Spread out table and its cloth,   bring the food.

    Fa ente, e mâ taſsil yedaic?
    dost not thou wash thy two hands?

A. Ei naᵀam, aſsilhê. (Yes, I wash them.)

M. Yâ Baᵀras, jieb eḷ ᵀaxt wa el ibrieq. Dawwirhê, Ḫatte'
   O Peter, bring the basin   jug. Carry them round until

    coll man yoried yaſsil yedaih, fa yaſsilhe.
    whoever wishes to wash his hands, may wash them.

    Teᵀâl ila honâ, yâ qasies! Iqteribou, jemieᵀcom.
    Come hither, O priest! Approach all of you.

    Wa ente, yâ râhib Simᵀân, e fa lâ (mâ) teteqaddam?
    monk Simeon, dost thou not advance?

S. Lâ! yâ seiyidna. Lâ toˤwâkiʌni,   ana   mâ
    our lord. Do not reprove me, I (am) not

ˤêcil semien.
eating fat (*gras*).

M. Ah! leix' mâ qoltoh liya qablan? Conna ᵀabakna
   why didst not tell it to me before? We would have cooked

    lee xaiˤ min eḷ semac. S. Lâlâ! mâ yaḪtêj.
    fish.   is not needed (VIII.).

M. Rouḧ, yâ Fânous; jieb lina ⸱asel naḧl wa zeitoun.
   Go   bring   honey of bees   olives.

   Marḧabâ bicom, yâ mo⸱allimien. 'Colou wa ixrabou
   Welcome to you, O doctors!   Eat ye   drink ye

   bi kâ⸱urcom.   El̤ nehêr ⸱awiel, wa (el ḥamd lillâh!)
   at your liking.   The day (is) long   praise to God!

   el ꜥeel   ceθier.
   the food (is) plentiful.

   Hel teꜥcol, yâ qasies, min el méxwiey?
   Eatest thou, O priest, of the roasted?

G. Min mexwiey mefroum,   faꜥinna eꜥcol.
         hashed (minced) verily I eat.

M. Cobb, yâ   mo⸱allim Zeitoun! ⸱ala heᴅêc el ʒaḧn
   Overturn (pour out) Doctor Olivier, upon that   dish

   min qar⸱ maḧxiey, ḧéᴅe el ḧalieb bil̤ toum.
   of gourd stuffed, this   milk with garlic.

Z. B'ism illâh! yâ seiyidi.

M. Jieb, yâ Ba⸱ras min   ⸱and   el̤   senbousqiey,
   Bring   from the *shop* of the confectioner,

   el kârouf el maḧxiey.
       lamb   stuffed.

B. Fânous râḧ li yeꜥkoᴅoh.   S. Hêhou jâyi bihi.
   Stephanos is gone to take it (get it).   coming

M. Ḧo⸱⸱oh fil wasa⸱.   N. Râyiḧatoh melieḧa.
   Put down midst.   Its odour

G. Wa el Ṭoṭma aḥsen.   M. Hel ente teʕrif ṭoʕmatoh?
   the taste is better.   Knowest thou its taste?

G. Lâ liḷ sêʕa : lâcin ana ḥastebtoh hêceʌê.
   Not yet :   but I   computed it thus.

M. 'Koʌ, wa ʌouqoh!   G. Ah! Ḣaqqaten! hêʌe hou ʕecl el
   Take   taste it.   verily! this is food

   moʕallimien. Yâ, eix' ḥalâwetoh!
   of doctors.   what its sweetness!

M. Eix' teᶻcol, yâ moʕallim Zeitoun?

Z. Ana fa eᶻcol yâknie,   eᶻcol waraq-a-dâliya,   eᶻcol
   I, why, I eat (ragout,)   leaf of vine,

   senbouseq, wa min jomlat kairât,   elleti toʕʕuihe
   patties   (any) among good things, which thou givest

   linâ biḷ ziyâda.   M. Wa ente, yâ moʕallim Ṣalieb?
   us in excess.   O Doctor Lacroix?

Ṣ. Ente, yâ seiyidi, aʕʕait   liya farrouja, wa ana ʕâmil
      hast given me a chicken,   I (am) making

   texrieḥ   ʕuẍâmiho.   M. E fa teʕrif ʕala 'l texrieḥ?
   dissection of its bones.   knowest about

Ṣ. Texrieḥ el laḥm el maʕbouk, fa   ana ʕârifoh.
   Dissection of meat cooked,   why!

M. Li naxouf xaʕâratec fie texrieḥ hêʌe el kârouf.
   Let us see thy cleverness in carving this   lamb.

Ṣ. Lâ! ente ḣaʕʕait (ḣaʕaʕt) yedec ʕalaihi (hast put).

Cemmil xoflec   wa farriqoh liḷ   ẋoyouf.
Complete thy work   divide it to the guests.

M. Lâ! hêᴀe hou waʒuifa   lil   moϯallim   Nâȝur.
             this is   · a function for   Doctor   Victor.

Yedaihi qawieya. (His two hands (are) strong.)

N. Bism illâh! 'koᴀ   ente! qasemtoh   ϯalaie.
              accept (this piece)! I have apportioned it to thee.

M. Yâ hêᴀih el xoqfa! hêᴀa faqaϯ yecfieni (yoceffieni)
   O   this   slice!   suffices me

   yeumain. N. Iᴀe lee xaiᵉ zêyid, iqsimoh mâϯ el qasies.
   two days.   If thou hast   superfluous, share it with

M. Maϯqoul!   Bilḥaqq hou leᴀieᴀ, wa ϯoϯmatoh melieḥa.
   Wise (saying). In truth   its taste

   Mán, baϯd hêᴀe el ϯaϯâm, yeᵉcol bâdinjân, ϯamâϯuin,
   Whó, after these viands, eats melongene, tomatoes,

   ϯunab, borteqân? G. Hêᴀe colloh rieḥ wa mowaiya.
   oranges?   wind and water.

M. Wa eḷ rozz, e mâ teḥobboh? (dost thou not like it?)

G. Aḥobb eḷ coscosou; amma xouraba min eḷ rozz, fa mâ
   toϯjibni qaϯ. M. Wa ceif eḷ rozz bi ḥalieb?

G. Yâ ᵉakoui, jaiyid, iᴀe cên bi misc wa ϯanbar kâm.
                  excellent, if with musk   ambergris raw.

M. Xouf hêᴀe eḷ râhib el mescien, râẋu bil ϯasel wa eḷ zeitoun.
   See this monk   wretched, pleased with honey and olives.

G. Ya seiyidi, li coll xaiᵉ waqtoh (to everything its time).

Ƭandi, baƬӼ el auqât, tecfieni qarqouxa : amma, iᴧe
With me, some times, dry crust (biscuit) but, if

jâni xai˙ aЂsen (esteƬrif lee) lâ armieh lil cilâb.
comes *to* me I confess I do not cast it to the dogs.

M. Wa el ƬuӼâm (*bones*), e mâ termiehê? G. El ƬuӼâm hie

qarâqiex el cilâb, wa esnâni mâ yaqdirou Ƭalaihê.
the biscuits of dogs, my teeth are not competent

M. Hel esnânec qâdirien Ƭala'l baflâwa? G. Mâ aƬrif min
strong (enough) for cheesecake. I know not for

zemân : fa˙inna mâ jarrabtohom fie hêᴧih el Ђâje.
(long) time : for I have not tried them in this affair.

M. Axouf fiḷ sêƬa. Xiel (*Remove*), yâ Fânous, hêᴧe colloh,

wa jieb lina el baqlâwa. Eix' teqoul fie hêᴧe ?

G. Hêᴧe, fie ʒanni, aЂsen min el jobon.

M. Jarriboh. (Try it.) G. Yâ yâ! colloh soccer wa lauz.

A. Ђaqqaten! hêᴧih el baqlâwa Ƭaiyiba.

Hel Ƭameltomhê fiḷ dâr? M. Yâh lâ! El niswân e fa
Did ye make them? (Would) women

yaƬrifou yaƬmilou hêᴧe? Ƭabbâk eḷ sinjaq Ƭamelhê.
know to make cook of the flag (regiment?).

N. Bil Ђaqq, Ƭajieba ; jadiera bil sanâjiq.
marvellous ; worthy of the flags.

Z. Lâ bodd, yerouЂ maƽrouf ceθier fie Ƭamel miθl hêᴧe.
No escape! goes (vanishes) expense in making

M. Γarxain θelâθe   bil ecθar.   'Col minhe.
Two *or* three piastres at most.   Eat of them.

A. Yecfieni fa ʿccelt ccθier.   (I have eaten much.)

M. Taſsil yedaic.   BaTras! jieb el Taxt wa el ibrieq maT
Thou shall wash   bason   jug

el Ṣâboun, li naſsil yedaina. Wa ente, Fânous! jieb
soap   our hands.   bring

lina el qahwe. F. Wa el maîoun, e fa lâ ejieboh?
coffee.   metal dish.

M. Kalli fawâcih el noqla wa el molebbesêt
Leave fruits   dessert   sugar plums (sweetmeats)

wa qarṣ el jobon el Afranji; wa jieboh. Lâcin lâ tokalli
cake cheese   Yet do not leave

el barnak bila jarra, wala el qomqom bila Tarqiey.
filtering stand   nor   (retort) without arrack.

N. Ana (aqoul lec el Ḥaqq) bi ciθrat   ma xarabt min
I   from plenty (of) what I have drunk of

el Taraqiey wa xarâb, baqiyat nâr   fie miTdati:
arrack   sherbet, has remained fire stomach

fa elʿân morâdi en axrab mowaiya.
now my wish (is) a sup of water.

M. Lâ! kalli yejiebou lec qadaḥ min limonâda wa 'koᴀ lec
let (them)   goblet   take

loquaimat   selâᴧa.   Ya abouna Jarjes, e mâ toſanni
small mouthful salad.   our father   sing

lina xaiʾ ᴀel waqt? (to us something now?)

G. Ya seiyidna, min ein toried yaʔlaʔ el seut,   lemma
            whence   come forth sound (*nomin.*) when

   el baʔn melˤân?   Teʔrif enna barmiel melˤan mâ
      belly (is) full?   Knowest   barrel   full   not

   yaʔunm xaiˤ.   M. Lâlâ, hêᴀe mâ yemnaʔac qaʔ.
   tinkle   hinders at all.

G. Fa li ofanni iᴀen!   B'ism illâh!
   Let me sing then!

§ 10. TWO TRADESMEN.

M. Ahah! e mâ teqoum? eix' hêᴀe el nafas baʔd ʔolouʔ ul
            does not arise?   slumber   out-coming

   xams? hel ente marˤa, (*woman?* ˤem rajol? *or man?*)

   e mâ texouf el xams? qoum! aqoul lec.

N. Lâ towâkiᴀni.   Elbâriḧ   inni cont ʔand Ḧabiebi
   Excuse me!   The (day) past I was with my friend

   (ʃaduiqi, ʃâḦubi). Ecelna, xarabna, fariḦna wa

   qaʔadna ʔand el sofra (maˤida) ila' nuʃf il leil. Fa
   we sat at the tray? (table) till midnight

   ˤana mâ jiet ilâ honâ, illa   qarieb min el meˤᴀena.
      I   not came hither, except near the calling to prayer.

M. Melieḧ jiddan. El bâriḧ baʔaltom bi sebab el xarâb,
   Very good.   Yesterday ye idled by cause of drink

wa el yeum tebTalou bi sebab el naum. Bainama ente
to-day ye idle   sleep.   While thou

hêceʌe baTTal, mánou yaTmel xoflec?   mánou
so an   idler   whó   does   thy business? whó

yaHcom   dârac? e mâ lec marʿa wa aulâd? mánou
governs thy house?   a woman (wife).

yeesichom? mánou yoTTumhom? N. Ah! Rabbona
clothes them? whó feeds them?   our Lord

ceriem,   wa hou el modabbir. Hel yomcin yanse'
(is) generous   he is the director.   can he forget

kalâyiqoh? M. E fa mâ qâl fil citêb il Taziez:
his creatures? Hath he not said in the book precious,

"ITmel, wa ana osêTudac?"   N. MaTqoul. Lécin
Act   and I will aid thee?   Wisely said.

eix' aTmel? Ana Toul el esbouT fil xofl, wa teTabi bil
         I, length of week   business, my toil (is)

ziyâda. Θomm, e mâ esteHuqq en eʲkoʌ liya yeum, li
in excess.   do not I deserve to take for me a day,

afraH fieh wa eʲcol wa axrab maT el aʾsHâb?
that I may rejoice in it . . . . companions.

M. Sadaqt: xoflec   wa   teTabee _ ceθier.
Thou art right: thy business and toil (is) too much.

Yâ mescien, ceif yomcin taʾsbor Tala hêʌe colloh? Min
O unhappy! how canst thou endure against all this? Of

el   ṣabâH teqoum baTd TolouT el xams: baTd fasl
a morning thou risest after sunrise: after washing

el wejh wa el yedain, texrab el qahwe.

Baîdoh, terouḫ lil ḫânout (doccén). (to the shop.)

Ťöulima teqîod honêc, texouf el nâs wa toʃâḫub
As long as thou sittest there, companiest

(maî)hom. Te⁵koᴀ darâhim min hêᴀe wa min heᴀêc.

Waqt el ᴧohr te⁵col wa texrab melieḫ. Baîd el
îaʃr tefloq wa teqfol el doccén; wa
afternoon fastenest and padlockest the shop

lemma yexoufouc ⁵ehl dârec îala îatebet il bâb,
when see thee thy household at threshold

yoḫᴧur lec el ma⁵ida (sofra *Alep.*), îalaihe el ⁵ecl,
get ready table, upon it food,

kamse sitte jonous; te⁵col wa texrab maî jemâîatec ⁵ecle
five six kinds thy company food

îaiyibe, wa bil mehl. Wa⁵emma hêᴀe colloh teîab!
nice and at leisure. But all this (is) toil.

N. Ente taᴧḫac îalaiya. M. Lâ: bel etecellem bil ḫaqq.

N. Ana îârif ennec tetecellem bil ᴧaḫc. (speakest in ridicule).

Lêcin aîterif lec el ḫaqq; hêᴀe el solouc elleᴀi ente qoltoh
I confess truth procedure

ᴀel waqt, inni moteîawwad îalaihi. Wa⁵emma, bima
verily, I *am* used to it. But when

etelâqa ana maî el aʃḫâb, fa iᴀᴀêc innena ne⁵col, nexrab
I meet with comrades, then verily we eat, drink,

wa nenbásiî bi faraḫ aîʒam.
and relax ourselves with mighty joy.

M. Eix' hêᴀe el faraḤ el aᵗʒam? qoum! wâḤud yesteʿnec
What is this mighty joy? Arise! some one awaits thee

ᵗala'l doccên, wa morâdoh(en) yaxteri minnec jouk.
at the shop, his wish (is) to buy woollen cloth.

Teᵗâl, célimoh. Come and talk to him.

N. YaʒuḤḤ. Yâ walad, jieb liya Ḥawâyiji.*
It is right. Boy! bring me my clothes.

P. Eix' min Ḥawâyij? N. Aᵗtuini qamieja (qamieʒa)
What sort of clothes? Give me (camicia) a shirt

nâqiya, wa qonbâz diemiey min dâkil iḷ ʒandouq.
clean gown *futaine* (dimity-fustian).

ʒarwâli min jouk wa ʒadrieyati wa barnousi honâ ᵗala'l
My trowsers my waistcoat hooded cloak

Ḥabl. Ein eḷ tarbaux wa eḷ xâxe?
rope. Where is the red cap and muslin (turban)?

P. Coll xaiᵉ [wâjid] ḤâӠur. Hêhona el jawârieb.
Everything (ready) Here (are) stockings.

E taᵗlob xaiᵉ fairahe? Dost thou demand anything else?

N. Aᵗtuini el Ḥuzêm, wa el jezm el jadieda.
Give me belt boots new.

P. 'Koᴀhe: wa houheᴀe maḤrama. E teᵗtéj *zod*
Take it: lo here a kerchief. Needest thou more

(ezyad?) N. Lâ: jieb el maᵉ, li afsil wejhi.

P. Fiḷ séᵗa. Yesténec eḷ rajol. (The man awaits thee).

* Ḥawâyij, *necessaries*, is used for one's *baggage*, also for *clothes*.

§ 11. CLOTHIER AND HIS CUSTOMER.

N. E mâ naxrab el qahwe, ana wa ente, qablama nerouḤ?

M. Ah! daʈ nerouḤ bila xarb el qahwe. E mâ naxraboh fil̦ doccên? N. Yomein. Lâcin morâdi naxrab honâ.

M. Ana xarabtoh min el ʇabâḤ: hel ente teḤsobni ʇâyiman?

N. RouḤ, 'ko⌂ el miftêḤ wa imxi qoddâm, li tefteḤ el̦ doccên.

P. Ana râyiḤ.   N. Wa naḤna warâc.   M. Ilbis qabâ-c.*
   I (am) going.   We behind thee.   Put on thy robe.

N. Hel ilbis ellé⌂i   bil farwa?   M. Ceif lec Ḥâje bil farwa?
          that which fur?   need of fur?

   El yeum, el̦ sokouna ceθiere.   'Ko⌂ lec hê⌂ih el kafiefe.

N. Bism Illâh! narouḤ.   P. Selâm ʈalaic, ya sciyidi.

Q. ʈalaic el̦ selâm.   El têjir e fa marieẋ?   waʾilla fâyib?
               Is the merchant sick? or absent?

P. Lâ! hou hê⌂e jâyi warâya.
   here he is, coming behind me.

Q. Ceif jâyi?   Ana qâʈud honâ ʈala el qahwe fie istinzâroh
   How coming?   I (am) sitting   in expectation of him

   min miqdar sêʈtein.   Hel yeftèḤ coll yeum hêce⌂e?

P. Lâ.   Râsoh, hê⌂ih el leile, cên youjaʈoh xaiʾen; ʈala
     His head, last night, pained him somewhat

   xân (min xân) hê⌂e, mâ jiena ʈala 'l ʈâda. Hou hê⌂e
   jâyi.   Ana e fa mâ qolt lec?

     * *De Braine.* Perhaps it is Algerine, in this sense.

N. Lâ towâkiʌni. Ana marieš xaiᶜen, wa raqadt li hêde el
waqt. Q. ȢuḦḦatec! lêcin ɣomcin etꞮabtec biḷ ziyâda.
    Thy health! but possibly I tired thee

N. Lâ! *bil kiláf* (bel) ana hou elléʌi moꞮꞮub Ɪalaic, waᶜemma
    on the contrary, it is I that (am) tiresome to thee, but

ente istênaitni   zemân.
thou hast waited for me a (long) time.

Q. Ah! lâ ictirâθ minnoh; (mâ obâli).   Ente teꞮrif, enna
    (there is) no concern; I do not mind.   knowest, that

Ɪuiƌi qarieb; wa morâdi eᶜkod minnêc jouk, bihi
my festival (birthday) I wish to take   with which

aꞮmel qabâ.   N. Aḧmar? waᶜilla arjawân?
I (may) make   Red?   or   purple.

Q. Arjawân. N. Hou Ɪanƌi. Ya ꞯâli! jieb basꞮat jouk el
               It is with me. Ali! bring a strip of

arjawân. Eix' taqoul fie hêde el jouk? E mâ hou

melieḧ? Lau cên dort el mediena, mâ tolâqi miθliho.
    If you had gone round the city, you meet not its like.

Q. Melieh! qadd eix' eḷ ʌirâꞮ?   N. Bi sitte riyâlât.
    how much the ell?   At six dollars.

Q. Eix' hêʌe el celâm? teḦsobni faxieman bi coll xaiᶜ,
What is this saying? countest me simpleton

ceᶜinna ana fie ꞯömri mâ xoft jouk, illa hêʌe? Wa
as if I in my life never saw cloth but this?

hêʌe el jouk bi sittet riyâlât eḷ ʌirâꞮ!

N. Ѳemenoh hêccʌe, yâ seiyidi. Iʌe aradt têˤkoʌoh, 'koʌoh : awemâ (*or not*) teˤcoʌoh ? kallichi. Bil Ḫaqq, mâ tolâqi fil medicna collihe jouk miѳl hêʌe. Ȝöufoh (*its wool*) miѳl Ḫarier, wa launoh zêhi. Ah ! mă aḤsen el qabâ, like silk its hue gay. how handsome the robe elléti teʕmalhe minnoh ! (which you will make of it.)

Q. ȜaḪuiḪ, el jouk melieḪ ; lêcin el ѳemen fâli.

N. Coll xaiˤ yaḪriz seumatoh. (See Bocthor, Valoir.)
maintains ? its valuation (*claims, gets* its price ?)
Youjad fil bâzêr jouk bi riyâlain, wa youjad bi sitte riyâlât.

Q. Naʕam : lâcin ʌêlic aḤsen min hêʌe. . . . (better than.)

N. Ȝaddiqni, auʕâ min jouki hêʌe.
Believe me, it is inferior to this *my* cloth.

Q. E toried teˤkoʌ lec kamse riyâlât ? (wilt thou take—)

N. Lâ kạmse : liˤenni xaraitoh (ixteraitoh) bi ecѳar.

Q. Mâ yaḪitêj totʕub rouḪac, wala ana rouḪui. Akir
needs not, I tire thy spirit, nor I the end, last
el celâm, oʕʕui lec kamse riyâlât. Iʌe cont toried,
'koʌ el darâhim.   Incên mâ toried, fa ofettix liya
wâḪud   fairac,   yosʕufni bi Ḫâjeti.
some one other than thee, will aid me in my affair.

N. ʕala kâturac. Ya tera' toḪsin ˤemree !
At thy pleasure. I hope, wilt well-manage

Q. Leix' teʕmel maʕya hêceʌe ? bil Ḫaqq, ente ʕammâʕ.
Why actest with me thus ? In truth covetous.

N. Ṱase toried hedieya minni; fa 'koᴀ lec el jouk bila θemen.
   Perhaps   a present   the cloth without price.

Q. Là: bi darâhimi mâ toṪṪuini ieyâho; fa keif hêᴀe hedieya?
      for my money thou givest it not;   is this a present?

N. BaiṪ hêᴀe el jouk bi kamse riyâlât, e fa hou biḷ darâhim?
   To sell this cloth for five dollars, is that for money?

   Ṱala dieni, ixteraitoh ana fiḷ zemân il sêbiq bi kamse
   On my faith, I bought it myself in former time for five

   riyâlât: walâcin li'enna ente zebouni, wa ʒabart ṫalaiya
   dollars, but because   my customer,   waitedst

   hêceᴀe min bocra, 'koᴀoh bi kamse wa nuʒf.

Q. Ṱala ᴀimmeti mâ yeswa (*is not worth*) xai" ceθar min el
   kamse; wa'emma ezied lec eḷ nuʒf.

N. Cem toried min el eᴀrâṪ? Q. Kamset eᴀrâṪ. Qies melieĥ.
   How many ells wishest thou?   Measure (it)

N. Xouf! inni qistohe temâma; kamse. IqṪaṪ, ya walad,
   See! I have measured it   Cut, O boy!

   honâ, wa uṪwiehe: wa jemieṪ   eḷ θemen hou ʒebṪa
   here,   fold it: the whole of the price is

   wa ṫuxrien riyâl wa nuʒf riyâle ṫalaie liya, yâ seiyidi.

Q. Ṫaiyib; fa 'koᴀ el foroux. N. KâṪurac ṫalaiya.

§ 12. WITH A TAILOR.

Q. Morâdi, en tofaʒʒul wa tokayyiṪ liya hêᴀih el jouka.
   I wish you to cut out and sew for me this cloth.

Lâcin lêzim en teqieshê, wa tenzor imma yettefiq
But you must measure it, and look whether fits

miqdârhê li qâmeti. B. Cem min el eᴀroṮ tejieb liya?
its size to my stature. How many ells bringest ?

Q. ArbaṮ eᴀroṮ. B. Ȝadaqt. ˁEmma mâ yeefie qaṮ.

Q. Qadd eix' taṮlob fauq min hêᴀe? How much...above this?

B. Aṯouz ezyad nuȜf ᴀirâṮ. (I need more than ½ ell.)

Q. Wa ṯandi ᴀirâṮ cêmil. (a whole ell.) Ɵomm inna eix'
têkoᴀ ente ṯala hêᴀih el ciswa? (for this garment.)

B. Mâ aqdir aṮlob aqall min kamse wa arbaṯuin fuᴧᴧa.
I cannot ask less than 5 and 40 silver.

Q. ȜaḤḤ el ˁemr; fa abṯaɵ lee bi yed kâdimi el nuȜf ᴀirâṮ el
All right I send my servant

nâqiȜ. E toried oˁweddi lee aiᴧan ciswati el ṯatieqa,
deficient I hand to thee my old garment

lecei ṯala miɵlihê teṯmel el jadieda?

B. Lậ yaḤtêj: aṯrif qiyâsee: wa ofaȜȜul lee libs aḤsen min
Is not needed: thy measure: cut out a dress

hêᴀe. Lêcin aqoulee:—Fie ṯömri ana mâ kayyaṮt
But I tell thee: In my life I never sewed

arkaȜ minnoh. Wa el *colfa*,* e fa toṮṮuihe liyâ? waˁilla
a cheaper than it. trimming(?) givest it? or

aḤöṮṮhe min ṯandi, wa teroddhe liya baṯdoh.
shall I put it from my own, and thou repay it . . . ?

* Additional materials,—*superfluity*.

Q. Wa eix' hêᴀe el eolfa zod (biḷ ziyâda)?

B. E mâ teȋrif, ennoh minxân eḷ sejâf lâ bodd min θelêθ
knowest not, that for the flounce, no escape from 3

eᴀroȋ aȾlas, bi ſarxain el ᴀirâȋ: hom sitte ſoroux: fa
ells of satin, at 2 piastres an ell: six piastres:

eḷ ezrâr wa el qaiȾân ſarx: hêᴀe sebȾa: wa el Ḧarier
buttons   laces, (loops)   seven   silk

robȋ ſarx: iᴀen, colloh sebȾa ſoroux wa robȋ. (7¼.)

Q. Mâ kammant qaȾ hêᴀe el tekmien: wa'inni Ḧasebt, en
I never estimated   estimate: but I counted to

oȋȾui lec, maȾada el jouk, kamse wa arbaȾuin fuᴙᴙa,
give thee, beside the cloth, five   forty

wa terodd liya el eiswe cêmile mocemmale.
you give back to me the garment complete, finished.

B. Lâ yomein.   Fauq teȾabi wa eirâya, fa hel aȾȾui lee
Above my toil   wages,   I give thee

aiᴙan sebȾa θemâniya ſoroux? Ente mâ taʒonnoh wala
also   7 or 8 piastres? Thou dost not think it, nor

toriedoh minni. (wish it from me.)

Q. Hel min el lêzim, en teḦöȾȾ eḷ sejâf? (to put the flounce.)

B. Eiwa lêzim: lâ bodd minnoh. Wa min farwa, fa cên
Yes, necessary: no escape from it. And of fur

aθman minnoh min aȾlas, in ʒâr melieḦ wa jemiel.
more costly of it than satin, if it were good

Eix' toried minni, ya seiyidi.

Q. Aḥsen en teḥöṭṭ el aṭlas, wa ma qolt liya tewa (*just now*). Fa arodd lec el θeman. (I will repay the cost.)

B. Ana bi kidmatec (*at thy service*). Wa maṭ el selâme.

§ 13. A STATIONER WITH A PAPER MERCHANT.

A. Selâm ṭalaic, yâ kawâja! (O sir!)
B. Ṭalaic el selâm, ya seiyidi el xeik! (*sheikh*.)
A. Ṭandac xai² cêfiṭ (waraq)? B. Ṭandi.
A. Qadd eix' el corrâs?
How much the (quire—De Br.)
B. Onʒor el cêfiṭ qabla, wa baṭdoh etecellem.
Look at the paper first, and afterwards I will speak.
A. Melieḥ: ḥull el ʒorra.   B. Hêʌe hou el cêgiṭ: e mâ
Good! untie the bundle.   This is the paper:

hou ḥasen? A. Maṭloum, jamiel: fa eix' ṭala el corrâs?
B. Ḥoṭṭ liya micya wa ṭaxara foroux, wa 'koʌ lec θelâθa
wa sitten corrâs. (110 *piastres*, 63 *quires*.)
A. Mâ yaʒuḥḥ hêceʌe: bel li neterâbaṭ awwalan ṭala coll
It is not well thus: but rather let us covenant first about each

rizma, θomm baṭdoh etefeccer cêm wâḥuda e²kod minhe.
packet, afterwards I will consider how many I take.
B. Ṭala kâṭurac: iʌen, toṭṭuini farxain ṭala' el corrâs: fa
tejid ṭaxara fie colli rizma. (you will find 10 in . . .)

A. Mâ yaḥtemil : wa hou ḥudd ḥusêbec el sêbiq, bil collieya.
   It is inadmissible   against thy former reckoning, entirely.

   Ṭala ʒanni, farx wâḥud ecθar minma testeḥuqq.
   In my opinion, a single piastre (is) more than it deserves.

B. Lâ : faʿemma mâ yokalliʿsni : bel ras mâloh ecθar min el
   No : but it does not clear me   cost price is more than the

   farx el wâḥud. Oḥsob ente, qadd   eix   tocellif
   single piastre.   Compute thyself, how much it cost

   min Bendiqieya ila honâ.
   from Venice to this place.

A. Ente taʿrif, fa ʿente teʿtebir resmâlac : lêcin mâ ʿalaiya,
   knowest   considerest : but it does not rest on me,

   en etedâkal fie ʿemarac : ana el xâri. Iʌe aradt
   that I meddle in thy affair : I (am) the buyer. If thou wish

   tebieʿ, fa bieʿ liya. Iʌe lem toried, fa qoul liya :
   "Yonʿum Allâh!"   Fa eʿkoʌ kamse rizem, fie coll
   rizma ʿaxara cerâries ; wa oʿṭuie θemânien farx.

B. Bil ḥaqq, ente mâ, ʿömree, xoft cêfiʿ aḥsen min hêʌe.

A. Mâ raʿeit aḥsen : ʿʃaḥuiḥ : lêcin xoft ceθier miθloh. In
   xaʿ 'llâh, yeji liya el nafʿ elleʌi jâ liya min fairoh.

B. 'Koʌ lee aiʌan kamse rizem. (take 5 packets more.)

A. Lâ : hêʌe yeefi liya. Baʿdama estenfiʿ minnoh, wa yeji
   liya el folous, eji lee marra ʿokra'. ʌel weqt mâ baqi
   ʿandi darâhim bil eefâya. Lâ : *wa* dieni !
   remains not . . . money . . .   by my faith !

B. Mâ obâli. (Mâ ꞇalaiya. Mâ ꞇala bâli.) aꞅbor ꞇalaic.
I do not care. (It is not on my mind.) I wait for thee.

A. Fa cem xehr taꞅbor?   B. Aꞅbor ꞇalaic xehrain.
    how many months wilt wait?   2 months.

A. E᷾koᴀ, incên taꞅbor sittet axhor. (if . . . 6 months.)

B. Sittet axhor! cix' min el celâm hou hêᴀc?

A. Lêcin mâ okalliꞅ nefsi fic xehrain. Min ein ajieb el
But I do not clear myself in 2 months. Whence

    θemanien riyâl el okra'? El mablaſ mâ hou min el
    the 80 other dollars? The sum is not (a matter) to be

    mostehên.   Lâlâ! Mâ yomcin; Aqall ma yecoun,
    made light of.   It cannot be; the least that...

    aꞇlob θelêθ axhor. B. Ismaꞇ liya. Aqoul lec ꞇarieq
    e᷾kar, aɦisen min hêᴀc. Aqsiꞇ ma bainana, wa ente
    another way,   Apportion what is between us

    toufieni el dain bil qosouꞇ. A. Fa ceif yaꞅlaɦ bainana?
    shall pay me instalments.   shall it be settled

B. Aqoul lec. Ente ꞅaɦub doccên, wa mâ yeji lec el darâhim
       master of a shop,   comes   money

    dafꞇa wâɦuda, bel qalielan qalielan, ꞇala qadar el baiꞇ
    single stroke, little by little,   according to sale

    wa el xira'. Emma, li᷾en noshil ꞇalaina el ꞇarieq,
    and purchase. But, for that we may ease to us the way,

    li naqsiꞇ el θemanien riyâl, ɦaqq el kamse rizem el
    let us distribute the 80 dollars (due to) the 5 packets

θêniya, ᵗala θemâniya ſarx coll el jomᵗa: wa baᵗd xehrain wa nu𝒮f fa lâ yabqa liya ᵗandec xai', El ſoroux eḷ θemânien el oula', fa tedfaᵗhe hê▵ih eḷ sêᵗa. Eix' teqoul fie hê▵e?   A. Melieḣ.

§ 14. SPECIMEN OF PROSE WITH FEW VERBS.

Teḣt   jins   el   ᶜibl   toujad   nauᵗân; eilê-homa
Under the genus of Camels are found 2 kinds; each of the two

ceriem   eḷ   ᵗabaᵗ,   ᵗaჳuim eḷ nafᵗ   li soceên   barrieyat
generous in stamp, immense of utility, dwellers desart

Afrieqieya, wa bilâd el ᵗarab wa ſairahe min el bilâd elleti
of Africa   country   Arabs others than it of districts which

teḣt kaᵗᵗ eḷ Seraᵗân. Fa eᶜḣad homa eḷ Dohêmij, — wa
under line Cancer.   one of the two Bactrian Camel

hou ▵ou senâmain. Fa el eᶜkar el Jemal,—fa hou ▵ou
       two humps   other   Camel   endowed with

senâm wâḣud, wa aᵗჳam qouwaten min eḷ Dohêmij, wa
one hump   mightier in strength than

ecθer   wojoudan minnoh.
more abundant in existence than he.

Wa lil Jemal ra's 𝒮aſier biḷ nesebat ila ᵗuჳm joθθetoh,
    camel has head small in proportion to great size carcass

wa o▵nân qa𝒮uirâtên, wa ᵗönq ᵗawiel, monḣani. Wa
  two ears   short   neck   long   flexible.

irtifâʔoh ila ʌirwat senâmoh naḫöu sitt aqdâm wa nuʒf.
elevation to top   hump   about six feet   half.

Wa laun wabaroh, fie qorb min el senâm, qàtim ; wa fie
    hue   shag   in neighbourhood of   dull, dim ;

sèʻir jismoh, launoh ceʻinna ḫömra kafiefe. Wa liho
rest body   as if   red   light.   he has

ʌenab ʕawiel wa manâsim mofarʕaḫa monxiqqa ; waleeinnehé
tail   long   pad-feet   distended   split   and yet they (are)

fair monfáʒula. Wa fie sêqoh toujad sitt ʕöqad. Wa liho
not separated.   his leg are found six knots.

miʕda   kâmise, fair el miʕd   el arbaʕ, elleti hie li coll[i]
a stomach fifth without stomachs   four which are to every

ḫaiwân mojtirr. Wa hou ʒabour ʕala 'l ʕaʕx wa el jouʕ,
animal ruminant.   he is patient against thirst   hunger

wa ʕala rafʕ   el aʕbâ   el θeqiele seiran serieʕan fie
        lifting (carrying) packages heavy a march   swift in

sefarât ʕawiele.
journeys long.

§ 15. NEWSPAPER EXTRACTS.

1. Qad ʒaherat ḫarieqa   fil xehr il mâɣu fie
   Already appeared a conflagration in the month past in

Ezmier ; wa bil rafm ʕan mobâdarat   il   ḫöcouma   li
Smyrna, and in spite of the hastening of the Government to

uʕfâihe, uḫteraq bihe miʻya wa kamsoun doccên wa
extinguish it, was burnt by it 100 and   50   shop and

baṯɅ maḫallêt.   Wa ceᴧêlic fiḷ xchr il
several places (blocks of houses). And likewise in the month

mȧᴧu qad ixteddat   el ṯawâṩuf   fie   xoṯout
past   became intense the gales (storms) on the coasts of

Rôdos; fa ᴧehib bi ˤeθ'rihê   baṯɅ eḷ   scfâyin.
Rhodes; vanished in their track a portion of the ships.

  2. Ṩaḫuifa   fie Filadelfia axhcrat,   naqlan
   A (newspaper) sheet in   has published by transcript

ṯan morêsela   waradat ileihe,   ḫusêb
from a correspondence (which) arrived to it a computation of

eḷ ᴧeheb el leᴧi karaj min Cêlifornia wa Austrâlia bi moddat
the gold which came forth from   the space of

il ṯaxar senien il ˤekiera: fa cên sebaṯ miˤya milyaun franc.
the ten years last   and it was 7   100 million

  3. El Matjar.   Jamieṯ el aṩnâf,   wa el esṯâr
       Commerce. All descriptions (of articles), and the rates

ṯala ḫâlihe,   lem tofraq xaiˤen ṯan el esbouṯ
according to their condition; did not differ at all from week

ul mȧᴧu; wa lâsieyima   woqouf el ḫarace   bi sebab
   past   especially the stoppage of movement (is) by cause

il amṯâr il fazierat, el leti hebaṯat fie hêᴧe el esbouṯ.
of the rains copious which have fallen in this week.

  4. Uṯlân.   Narjou el baṯɅ min el moxtericien, el leᴧien
     A notice. We entreat that part of the subscribers who

lilˤên lem   yadfaṯou θemen el jornâl ṯan hêᴧe el ṯâm,
hitherto have not paid the price of the journal (for) this year,

164   HANDBOOK OF MODERN ARABIC.

en yobâdirou bi uiṣâl ᴀêlic; li⁵ennoh qad   fât   el
that they hasten to present it; because already is passed the

waqt el moṱayyan liḷ daṱṱ.
time appointed for paying.

5. Inna el vâpour el Fransêwi *Seyyid-Nous,* ṱarrafnâcom
   As to the steamboat French   we informed you

ṱannoh sêbiqan,   enna sêḦuboh vâpour e⁵kar; li⁵enna
concerning it formerly that (is) towing it (*nom.*) another because

⁵êletoh cênet teṱaṱṱalat.   Θomma fehemna min qabiṱânoh,
its engine was disabled.   Next we learned from its captain

ennehom ṣallaḦouhe, wa ṣâr bihi   el cefâya   liḷ
that they have mended it, is become sufficiency (ability) for

sefar.   Fa sêfar nehêr eḷ sebet el mâᴵu.
the voyage.   it set off the day of Saturday past.

6. SêḦat el Ḧöboub motenaxxiṱa jiddan, wa qad taṱâlet
   Area (Market) grain(s) active (lively) very   have risen

esṱâr el Ḧunṱat il Muṣriey il tojjâriey min 32 ila 33 el
the rates of wheat   Egyptian   mercantile from   to

ceile.   El Ḧarier qaliel, lecinnoh   râyij:
measure (tub).   silk (is) scarce, but it (is) selling-fast

el beladiey min 170 ila 190 el oqqa.   El mânifâtoura, lem
    native   ounce.   manufacture did

tezel   esṱârhe motemessece, maṱ ennoh lem yezel el
not cease its rates holding fast, although ceased not the (cargo)

wârid mottâṣulan.
arriving continuous (the arrival continued incessant.)

7. Marsielia fie 4 Edâr.   Eḷ zeit;   ʿsâr ʿfalaihi jomlet
   Marseilles on   March. ₒ oil   a number

mabyouʿfât, wa lâsieyima liḷ ʿsâboun.   Eḷ simsin motenaxxiʿf
of purchases   especially for soap.   sesame   lively

jiddan, wa inbâʿf minnoh jânib ʿfaʒuim : wa qad taʿfâlet
         is sold   extent (quantity)   have risen

esʿfâroh. Fa hie bi suʿfr 60.
its rates. it (is) at rate

8. Janâb Adâbizêdeh xaraʿf   bi ʿfamel xarâcet
   His honour   has begun to make a partnership

cerkânet   fazl,   moqassem   resmâlhe   ʿfala 500
of a factory of spinning, being divided its capital over

sehman,   wa coll¹ sehm 2000 farxan.   Wa ibtedaʿ
lots (shares) every lot   piastres.   was begun the

ictitéb   el esmâ.   Wa hê∆ih eḷ xarâce lâ taqbal
enrolment of the names.   this partnership does not accept

xarieqan fair mostenʿtun fie Damaxq.   Wa el cerkâna tedour
a partner except domiciled   the factory is seeking

ʿfala el mây.
after water.

9. Jelêlet melicet Ingilterra qad kaʿtabat   fie Allemânia
   Majesty queen of England had betrothed in Germany

uḧda' binâthe   li ʿemier Hesse Darmstad ; wa el Lôrd
one of her daughters prince

Palmerston ḧaⅾar   li Bâries, wa isteqâm   bihe arbaʿf wa
                was present at Paris, (pop.) stayed there 4

ʿtuxrien séʿfa bi moḧâdaθét ceθiera.
  20   hours in interviews many.

10. Veniesia wa nawâḧuihe qad woδuʈat biḷ taḧ'ṣuinât
    Venetia   its precincts   are placed   fortifications

il metiene, wa‛in   tecon lem taʒher ʈala eḷ Numsé
substantial, although has not appeared   to Austria

hi‛yat ḧarb fie Iʈâlia.
a case of war *against* Italy.

11. Sardienia ‛ellafat jaixain,   el wâḧud ittéjah li
    has made up two armies;   the one   fronts to

nâḧuyat el Mincio bi ri²êset el jinerâl Marmora, wa eḷ θêni li
the side (frontier) headship general   the second

nâḧuyat el Bô bi riyéset Cialdini wa jinerâlain   fairoh.
the Po   two generals beside him.

Wa qad ‛omirat kamset ʈaxara firqa min jonoud, el mo-ḧâfaʒat
              are under command 15 detachment troops National

el ‛ehlieya, biḷ tewejjoh ila marâciz moktelifa.
Guard   to front   centres (sites) diverse.

12. Beirout.   Mesê el *kámis* el mâδu, qad istedʈa' Ḧaδrat
               Evening of Thursday past   invited (*nomin.*)

ṣâḧub eḷ daula   Fouâd Bâxâ janâb   ma‛mourie
owner? of lordship   their honours (*accus.*) the legation

wa qanâṣul jenerâlieyat eḷ dowal il fakiema lil ʈaxâ. Wa
   Consuls General of the Great Powers to supper.

cénet waliema ḧâfila.   Qaδouhe bi colli sourᵘʳⁱⁿ.
banquet fully-attended.   They ended it with all joy.

13. Wa qad ʈayyanat daulatoh   nehêr el iθnain
    appointed his lordship (*nom.*)   (*accus.*) Monday

wa nehêr el *kamies* min coll¹ esbouṬ li mowâjahet ro'osê el
    Thursday of every week to meet the chiefs of the

milel wa a'sḤâb el ma'sâliḦ wa el daṬâwi. Wa se-yetexarra-
sects   men of business   causes.   they will be

foun ledaihi min el   sêṬat il sêdise Ḥatte' el sêṬat il
honoured (with interview) hour sixth until

têsiṬa : wa yadkoloun   bi moujib il   noumerô el leti
ninth   they will enter by virtue of the *numero* which

toṬṬâ   lihom   Ṭala el bâb.
will be given to them at the door.

  14. Risêle min Marsielia fie 28 el mâẊu toṬlin enna el
     A dispatch from Marseilles of the past notifies that

fier el Ṭâmm fie Franse ittejih ila   hedou min   jihet
general opinion   France turns its eye to tranquillity in respect

netiejet   moqâbalet   Varsouviâ : wa 'enna hêẠih
to the result of the personal meeting at Warsaw

el moqâbala intehet fie 26 el xehr ; wa enna el uṬlânât el
     was ended VIII. of the month   the notices

siyêsieya   mo'umina.
political (are) confident.

  15. El tejrieda el Fransêwieya fie Côxin Ṡuin qad
      expedition   French   Cochin China

temellecet   fie 13 Niesên Ṭala mediena Mietou. Fa
had possession on the 13th April of the city

cênet   lihe   mercezen metienan.
it (*the city*) was to it (*the expedition*) for a firm centre.

16. Qad cotib min mediena Londrâ, enna el Lôrd Jôn
   Had been written from city London,

Rousel, nâӡur kârijieyat Ingilterra, qâl fie uĥda' jilsêt
   overseer of foreign affairs   said in one of the sessions

majlis   el   ʕömoum, ennoh lâ yara', wala
of the Assembly of Commons that he does not see not even

min jihe wâĥuda, kaʕara*n*, yakxi minnoh ʕala el ʒölĥ
from any side (any) danger from which he fears for the peace

el ʕâmm maʕ Ingilterra. Faᵌinna lâ mesiele, ʕanhe
   general with   In fact (there is) no question from which

yomcin   en yenjim el kaʕar.
it is possible that danger may arise.

17. Risêle min Corfou, uĥda el jezêyir el sebʕ, aʕlanat
    A dispatch   one of the seven islands   has notified

bi intixâb qutêl ɫain ᵌehêli el   mediena
outburst combat between the families (population) of the city

wa   ʕasêcir el mo-ĥâfaӡat il   Inglieziеya; ᴀehib
and the soldiers of the guard (garrison) English; in which

bihi ʕuxroun jerieĥan min el farieqain. Wa ᴀêlie fie 21 Eyâr.
came off 20 wounded from the two parties.   May.

18. El akbâr el ᵌekiera. Akbâr Tourien toʕlin, enna el
       news   last.   News of Turin notify

jaix el Iʕâliâni woÃuʕ ʕala qadam il ʒölĥ. Wa lâ raib
army   is placed upon a footing of peace. no strife (*doubt*)

enna ᴀêlie daliel ʕala nieyat   jelêlet il melic Victour
is a proof for the intention of the majesty of king

Ṭamânou‛el Ṭala dawâm iḷ Ṩölḥ wa eḷ selâm.   Wa li hêᴧe
Emmanuel for continuance   therefore
irtêḥat   el efçâr   min jihet ḥarb fie Iṭâlia.
gained repose (men's) thoughts in respect to war

19. Risêle min Tourin toṭlin, enna el Qônt Cêvour, nâʒur
kârijieyat Iṭâlia, qad waqaṭ fie Eyâr marieᴧan. Ѳomm
foreign affairs   fell   in May sick.   Next
tewâradat el akbâr   bi izdiyâd   marᴧoh; ḥatte'
kept arriving news (nom.) with increase of his disease until
akbarat   risêle fie 6 ḥazierân, ennoh qad teweffa' fie
reported a letter (nom.)   June   departed in the
Ṩabâḥ ᴧêlic el yeum.
morning of that day.

20. Inna mausim el aṭlâl   jaīyid   fie coll¹ mecên.
    season (crop) produce (is) excellent in every place.
Wa el ma‛moul,   enna esṭâr el ḥunṭa se-tecoun bi rakâ
the thing hoped (is) that rates of wheat will be in cheapness
Taʒuim,   lem tenteʒuroh   bilâdona   fiḷ
vast, which has not seen?   our country (nom.) in
senien il ‛ekiera.
the last years.

21. Ce ᴧêlic mausim el ḥarier jaiyid: innama el xarâniq,
    So too the season of silk   only?   cocoons
esṭârhe el‛ên bi ṭain iḷ nozoul; wa hie min suṭr 20 ila 23 el
    at present crisis of decline   rate
oqqa. Wa el ḥarier el beladiey 210.
ounce.   native

22. Lâ yokfa', enna el Qônt Cêvour qad teweffa' fie 6
   It is no secret, that Count   departed life

Ḫazierân biḷ sêꞎat iḷ sêbiʇa min eḷ ꜟabâḫ fie mediena Tourin.
June   hour   7   morning

Wa li hêᴧih el moꜟuibat il mow꜔ellima qad istafraqat Iʇalia
   at this   affliction   painful   is plunged

bi꜔esrihê bi aθwâb el Ḫudâd, el leᴧi bihi xâreche
in entirety in garments of mourning wherein shares with her

baqyat eḷ xoʇoub aiᴣan: li꜔enna faqd (foqoud) hêᴧe el
the rest of the peoples also   because the loss of this great

ʇaᴣuim qad ꜔eθθar fie coll il qoloub; ḫatte' inna aʇdâ
(man) has made a print on all hearts; so that verily the foes of

ittiḫâd Iʇâlia nefsehom aᴣherou el ꜔esef, bil ixtirêc
the union of Italy themselves displayed sorrow in partnership

maʇ benie' waʇanhom, ʇala faqd ᴧêlic eḷ xehim.
with the sons of their home at the loss of this energetic (man).

El꜔ên yaʇrif ꜔ehl   el   ʇöꜟr   miqdâr
Now knows the people (nom.) of the age the scale (accus.)

faᴣloh   wa semou   himmetoh   bi teqaddom
of his merit and loftiness of his purpose by the progress of

bilâdoh: fa꜔inna cênet afcêroh el ꜔ekiera (wa hou ʇala
his country: and in fact were his last thoughts (while he (was)

firâx iḷ nizêʇ) mottejihe   li ꜟalâḫ   bilâdoh wa
on the bed of agony) turned towards the good order of

ziyâdat   nejâḫuhe.
the increase of its prosperity.

23. Majlis   Vienna qad ʿecced   uṭâlet   el
    Assembly of Vienna   had confirmed prolongation of

ṣölḥ min   jihet   Iṭâlia : fa wejh aṭmâloh ila el uṣlâḥât
peace on the side of   aspect of its deeds (is) to reforms

il mâlieya, wa   uṣlâḥ   kalal   bilâd   il Majâr.
financial and the reform of disorder of the country Magyars.

24. Inna daulat Fransê qadd aqarrat bi maṭrifat
    dynasty of France has avowed its acquaintance* with

memlecet   Iṭâlia, cema axher   ᴀêlic Ṣaḥuifat
the kingdom of Italy, as has published (acc.) newspaper

el Patrie wa el Mônitour.   [* i.e. has recognized.]
(nom.) of

25. El gazettet el resmieya fie Vienna axherat   qarâra
          gazette   official   has published a statement

min   nâẓur   mâliyat el Nimse,   yoṭlim enna fâyidat
of the overseer of finance of Austria (which) notifies   interest

el qarᴅ ul ʿehliey todfaṭ min baṭd Niesên bi Ṭömla(?) fuᴅᴅuiya.
of the national debt shall be paid after April in coin   silver.

26. Binâʿan ṭala ʿemr Ḥaᴅrat Ṣâḥub el naẓârat il jaliele,
    In pursuance of the order of   oversight august

qad modd   firṭ   min silc il telefrâf   ila serâyâ el
  is extended a branch   wire of telegraph   palace of

maʿmourieyat   il mosteqilla,   liʿejl il mokâbara   maṭ el
the Commission plenipotentiary   communication

Ḥöcoumet   il senieya fie Damaxq bil mawâdd il resmieya.
Government   sublime   on matters   official.

27. E‛ḣad ᶜölemâ Prousia (Borousia) qad qaddam, baᶜd el
    One of the savans of Prussia   has presented

baḣaθ,   ila   jamᶜuyat   el maᶜârif   fie Berlin, ᶜadad
research to the Association of *Connaisances*   the number

xoᶜöub   il corʻet il ʻerΔuiya.   Fa qaddam el maᶜdal,
of the people of the terrestrial globe.   average(?)

el leΔi aᶜᶜâ-h, bi milyâr   wa miʻyetein   wa θemâniya wa
which he gave, 1000 million two hundred   eight

θemânien milyeunan. Θomma ḣaseb   el anwâᶜ el
eighty   million.   Then he computed the kinds (races)

insênieya bil inqusêm.
human   separately.

28. Uᶜlân. Noᶜlin ila' el jomhour, enna el kawâjâ
    A notice. We notify to the public   the monsieur

ᶜabd Allâh Ḣasoun el bâriᶜ fie fenn   il taʃwier   bil
                                who excels in the art of delineating with

yed,   wa el monfárid bil ittiqân hêΔih el ʃanâᶜa bi hêΔih
the hand the unique in the perfection of this profession

el bilâd,—mosteᶜudd li ᶜamal collⁱ maᶜloub yoqaddam
        (is) ready to perform every demand (which) is presented

liho min el taʃâwier il   moktelifa. Wa ce Δêlic, youjad
to him of drawings (paintings) diverse   So too,   is found

ᶜandoh, teḣt el ᶜalab, ᶜudda min el taʃâwier il lâzima lil
        under demand a number of drawings necessary

cenêyis wa lil boyout. Wa hou, ᶜada ᶜan ittiqân
churches   houses.   besides the perfection of his

ṡanâṫatoh, yabieṫ bi suṫr rakuiṡ.   Fa man   arâd   bi ṫalab
workmanship sells at a rate cheap.   whoever wishes to demand

minnoh   xai⁺en,   li   yaḣᴅur   ila   meeteb
of him   (any) thing let him   present himself at the office

ṡaḣuifatna.
of our paper.

29. Ḣarieqat Tooley Street, el leti naxiyat fie Londra fie
    The conflagration of   which arose

22 Ḣazierân, eénet lem tezel motewâṡala(ten) li   Ḣadd 1
   June   did not cease continuing   to the limit of 1st

Temouz fie ma bain arbaṫat eswâq, Ḣaiθoma* eénet ibtedat.
July   between four   streets where   it had begun.

30. Marsielia fie 6 Temouz.   Lâ axfâl ṫala el Ḣarier.   El
    Marseilles on 6 July.   No dealings in silk.

qarᴅ el ṫoθmâniey 77.
Ottoman loan

31. Inna Ḣaᴅrat ṡâḣub-el daula Dâoud Bâxâ, leilet el
arbaṫâ il mâᴅuya, ejâb   iltimês   el kawâjâ Jarjis Madwar,
Wednesday   accepted the entreaty of Mr. Georgius

fa xarraf   menziloh   lil ṫaxâ.   Wa eénat leile zéhiya bil
honoured his dwelling   supper.   a night gay with

anwâr wa élét   el ṫarb :   fa qaᴅat   daulatoh
lights   instruments of emotion ended (it) his lordship (*nom.*)

---

* Ḣaiθoma, *wherever*, is classical; but Ḣaiθ, *where*. Catafago gives Ḣaiθoma, *where*, which seems to be common, but less correct.

mesroura(ten) bi ma teqaddam lihe min el kadâmât.
delighted with what was presented to (it) of services.

32. Inna el̤ zienat el leti ʽSârat fil Istênat el Ṯalieya, bi
    As to adornment which was in Sublime Place, on

forʽSat el jolous el̤ seʽTuid el homâyouniey, cênat
occasion of the sitting (on throne) happy imperial, it was

ʽTala fâya ma yecoun min el behjat, el leti aʒherathe
extremity of what may be of delight displayed

jemieʽT el ʽehêli min el milel il moktelifa fie jamieʽT xawâriʽT
all the families of the sects diverse in all the roads

el Istêna wa maḤallâthe wa nawâḤuihe dâkilan wa kârijan;
places precincts within without

Ḥatte' cên ranien el afrâḤ wa el̤ sorour yowâʽSul el ʽefâq
so that echo (tinkle) of joys delight reached horizon

mokbiran bi afrâḤ el ʽommat, el leti lem yecon nauʽT min
declaring joys nation, which there was no kind of

meserrât, illa wa aʒheratoh bi ibtihêj ʽTaʒuim.
joyfulness but it displayed it with mighty glee.

33. Nehêr el eʽḤad fie 7 Temouz, qad jaʽ ḤaӠrat ʽSâḤub el̤
    The day of Sunday July came

daula QabuʽTân Bâxa ila menzil Ḥaӡrat sefier daulat
Gate-holder Chief lodging ambassador

Ingilterra el fakiema, Sir Henry Bulwer; (el leᴧi uʽTterâh
mighty (on whom supervened

marӠ lêzemoh el firâx;) lecei yeftâqid
illness (which) *caused* him to keep his bed) to inquire after

aḣwâl   Ṡuḣḣatoh min ladon ḣaᴣrat iḷ ᴀêt iḷ xâhênieyat il
the state   health on the part of   personage   regal

jeliela.   ʿEmma ḣaᴣrat eḷ sefier fa cén mamnounan jiddan li
august.   But   ambassador   obliged   at

héᴀe el iltifât il ʿaᴣuim; wa terejja ḣaᴣrat Ṡâḣub eḷ daula
   attention   besought

QabuTân Bâxâ, en yoqaddim texeccorâtoh wa mamnounieyatoh
   present   his thanks   obligation

ila jânib   il ʿarx il molouciey; cema rawâh morâsil
to the side of throne   royal   as narrated it a correspondent

min el Istênat il ʿalieya ila jornâl Esmier.
from Sublime Place to journal Smyrna.

34. Aḣwâl   Ameriece lem tezel bil irtibêc   il ʿaᴣuim
   Circumstances of   continued in entanglement   vast

min jihet il ḣarb bain el janoub wa eḷ ximâl. Wa lilʿen
in respect to the war   south   north.   hitherto

lem   yeterajjah   eḷ naṠr li eʿḣad, wa leis siwa'   el
did not preponderate   victory   there is nothing *but*

aᴣrâr el jesiema lil farieqain, el leti   laḣaq   teʿθierohe
huge losses   two parties of which has reached the impress

bi ecθar aqsêm el corʿe, li sebab   taʿʿuil   il
to most parts of the globe by reason of the disabling of the

matêjir il moteʿalliqa maʿ tile el bilâd.
commerces connected with   that country.

35. Maḣâcim   Inglieziеya. Inna el ḣumâr, lâ yejib
Courts of Justice English. As for the ass, not behoves

en naθqol ʕalaihi ecθar min el insên.   Wa liᴧêlic, teḥarracet
that we load on him more than   therefore was stirred

ɼairat   el   ʕabaʕuiya Clark fie eˁḥad   eswâq   Londrâ,
the zeal of the policeman   in one of the streets of

Ḥaiθoma   naʒar Ḥumâran mescienan,   yaḥmil fauq
(Ḥaiθ, *where*) he saw an ass wretched (who) carries above his

ʕâqatoh Ḥumlan θeqielan. Wa maʕ   hêᴧe, fa cên ʕâḥuboh
strength load   heavy.   in spite of   his owner

(el mosemma' William Abbot) sêciban ʕala hêᴧe el Ḥaiwân
        named   pouring on this   animal

el mescien wâbilan min el ᴁarb il xadied ʕala raˁsoh wa
wretched   a shower of   beating   violent on   head

ʕuᴁâmoh wa janboh wa jamieʕ jawâriḥ jesedoh; Ḥatte' cên el
bones   side   all   limbs of body   until

damˁ yesiel minnoh min coll¹ mecên. Fa elqa' el qabᴅ ʕala
blood streams   place.   he laid   arrest

ʕâḥuboh Abbot; θomma meθθeloh   ˁemâm   el   qâᴅu.
his owner ;   then submitted him in presence of magistrate.

Fa seˁeloh   qàyilan:
he asked him saying:

(*Qâᴅu.*) "Li mâᴧe ˁcᴧᴧeit   hêᴧe el Ḥaiwân?"
          Why hast thou illused this animal?

(*Abbot.*) "Ceif   tosemmi   hêᴧe Ḥaiwânan? wa hou
           How dost thou name this an animal? and he is

Ḥumâr; lâ ecθar.
an ass; no more.

Q. " Wa aẓönn, enna el ecθar tewaḥḥoxan min el iθnain,
   I think, that the greater in brutality of the two

leis hou el ḥumâr.   Wa lêcin li mâᴀe   aujaîteho   bi hêᴀe
is not the ass.   but why hast thou pained him on this

el miqdâr?   Fa hèl bi hêᴀih el wâsiƮa yamxi ecθar?"
scale   Will he by this means walk more?

A. "Lâ! bel biḷ Ӿudd, cên yanâm.   Wa lêcin ana
    No: on the contrary, he went to sleep. Yet I did

mâ aujaîtoh."
not pain him.

Q. " Ente Ӿarabteho Ʈala raᵋsoh wa Ʈala ƮuӾâmoh,
     Thou didst beat him on his head and   bones

ḥatte sêl eḷ damᵋ min jirâḥoh."
until streamed   his wounds.

A. " Ah bâh! hêᴀe leis bi xaiᵋ Ʈala el ḥumâr. Fa ᵋinni
     Ah bâh! this is nothing   In fact I (am)

maujouƮ ecθar minnoh; liᵋenna imrâti   waledat,
pained more than he;   for   my wife has given birth

wa lem   taƮad   taqdir   en taƮmel Ʈamelan, maƮ enni
has not been longer able to do   work   although I (am)

bi fâyat il uḷitiyâj ila kidmethe.
in extreme need   of her service.

Ḥuinaiᴀin teqaddam   eḷ ӾabaƮuiya, wa qâl:
Just then came forward the policeman, and said:

" Yâ moulâᵋi? inna el ḥumâr, qaddamtoh
  master, as for the ass, I have presented him (brought

ila bâb il maḥcema.   Fa ʽin aradt en tefḥaʽṣoh,
him) to the door of the Court.   if thou wish to examine him,

qoum   bina,   li nanʒor bi eiy Ḥâle hou."   Wa lil Ḥâl
get up with us, that we see in what state he (is).   instantly

karaj   el   qâᴅu Cenouces, maṯ cêtim sirrihi wa collⁱ
went out the cadi   Knox?   with his secretary

mowaʒʒufeihi li ziyârat il Ḥumâr il mescien, el leᴀi cên
his functionaries to visit the wretched ass,   who was

bil jehd yestaṯuiṯ el woqouf ṯala qawâyimoh.   Wa Ḥuinima
scarcely able   to stand   on   his legs.   as soon as

rajaṯöu li mecênihom, qâl el qâᴅu ila el   moxtéci
they returned to their place   the (man) complained

ṯalaihi: " Ente   waḥx : fa ʽinnec bi collⁱ qasêwa wa
against :   Thou (art) a brute   thou   cruelty

faᴅab   ᴅarabt   hêᴀe el Ḥaiwân el mescien.   Fa aḤcom
violence didst beat   I judge

ṯaleic   biḷ   sijn   xehran : wa eteʽèssèf li ceuni
against thee with prison for a month   I regret at my being

lem aqdir ejid lèc quʽʃâʽʃan aṯʒam."
unable to find   a punishment greater.

Fa karaj   el   maḥcoum ṯalaihi ; wa hou yaqoul
went out the (man) judged against   he says

motemarmiran: " El Ḥumâr mâ hou xaiʽ : wa maṯ hêᴀe, fa
grumbling   is nothing   for all that,

ʽinni qad ᴅarabt   imràti ècθar ; wa lem   yoḤcèm
I have beaten my wife   no(thing) was judged

ȋalaiya,   illa   bi   θemâniyat eiyâm fil sijn."
against me, except with eight   days   in prison.

36. Yoqâl, enna el Ab el Moqaddas qad nâl   ʒuḫḫatoh
    It is said,   Father   Holy   has obtained his health

el têmma, wa   mozmiȋ   en yoḫâfuʒ ȋala siyâsetho, el leti
complete   he is hastening to attend to his administration

etbaȋhe(?) li   ḫadd   el'ên.
to the limit of now.

37. Inna Ḫaⱬrat ʒâḫub el seȋâda Θorya Bâxâ, moteʃarrif
       his honour, lord of felicity,   ruler, rector

el Qads   el xarief, qad qaddam   li   kidmat   il
of Jerusalem the noble,   has presented to the service of the

jonoud il xâhênieya baȋlain   wa jawâdain;   wa
troops   regal   two mules   two steeds (chargers)

qob(b)ilet teqaddametoh hêᴅih bi coll¹ maḫʒouʒuiy.
was accepted his present   happiness.

38. Inna Ḫaⱬrat ʒâḫub eṭ daula wâli Ezmier,   qad
                     governor of Smyrna

manaȋ   ȶabâȋat ȋaznat Armenieya,   ʒaharat   bil
has hindered printing poem?   (which) appeared

moddat   il 'ekiera bi tile el mediena, b'ism "El Zêhra"
space of time   latest   in that city, with name

li'enna cênet ȶobiȋat   bi doun istie'ᴅên   au rokʃa   min el
        it was printed without asking leave or permission

ḫocouma.
government.

39. Nehér el ĉᶻḤad fie 11 Ab, ᵻand eḷ sèᵻat il θêmina illa
        Sunday   August   hour   8th   all but
kamse daqâyiq, Ḥadaθat fie Ezmier rajfa qawieya min
  5   minutes   occurred   Smyrna shock strong
zelzelet il ᶜerẌ.
quake   earth.

40. Cotib min Eidien el celâm elᶻêti:—Inna el eθmâr
    Was written   discourse following fruits (crop)

eḷ tien tesquᵻ min el afꞋân dâyiman: wa qad qiel, enna nuꞋf
  figs drop   boughs always   it was said   half

el maḤꞋoul qad ᴧehib bi hêᴧih el wâsiᵻa; wa enna, el leᴧi
  crop   is gone   means   that   what

baqa, radi jiddan; wa coll hêᴧe, min el marẌ el leᴧi
remained, bad   (is) from the disease

istaḤwaz ᵻala hèᴧih el eθmâr.
has taken possession of this crop.

41. Eḷ simsim wa el qoᵻn bi Ḥâle jaiyida fil waqt
    sesame   cotton (are) in excellent condition

il Ḥâᴣur: innema rieḤ eḷ ximâl, el leᴧi hebb bi hêᴧe el
  present only wind   north   has blown

esbouᵻ, qad aᴣarr jiddan biḷ zeitoun, wa ceser ceθieran min
week   has hurt   olives   has broken much

afꞋânoh. (*his* boughs?)

42. El Ḥarr xadied jiddan, Ḥatte' ᶜinnoh lâ yoᵻâq; wa
    heat intense   so that even it is intolerable

zelèzil el ʿerḍ motewâṣule.   Wa qad axṭarna   bi θemâniya
quakes of earth continuous   we have felt   eight

rajfêt bi moddat sêṭât qaliele.
shocks space of hours few.

43. Sêḣat   el Ḧoboub motcḣassenat el aḣwâl.   El
Area (Market) of grain (is) improved

mânifâtoura lem tezel motenaxxuṭa : waʿemma mâl   el
manufactures   lively, active   goods of the

qabbân,   fa aqall ḣarace minhe.
large* scales, less movement of them.   * Heavy goods.

44. Jelâlet el Imperaṭöur Napôliôn qad tewejjah   min
    Majesty   has turned his face (*set off*)

Pâries ila Viexi fie Fransê ; wa qâbaletoh   el ʿeḣêli   bi
Paris   Vichy   confronted him the people

ibtihêj ṭaʒuim.
delight.

45. Akbâr Iṭâlia el janoubieya toṭlin bi qalâqil jadieda ;
    News   southern   inform   disturbances new

wa enna el jinerâl Cialdieni noṣub   qâyidan li jaix   il
   that general   is appointed leader   army of the

janoub : wa yeteʿemmeloun   enna ḣoẓouroh   fie Nâpoli
south   they consider (*expect*)   his presence in Naples

se-yohemmid el hiyâj.
will quell the uproar.

46. Lem yezel el uḍṭurâb motemeccinan fie aqṭâr
    Did not cease   commotion growing strong   regions

Ameriece ; wa lem tezel el ḥarb el ʿehlieya toheddid el
of America   war   domestic threatens

jamieʿ min el farieqain.
whole   two parties.

47. Inna ʿömdat bilâd el Majâr qaddamat li jelâlet Im-
    (*Diet*) of Hungary presented to Majesty

perâʿtour il̦ Numsê el ʿarẋ el moteẋammin teʿallobât
           Austria   address   containing   demands

bilâdihom : wa auʿadathom jelâletoh bi uʿʿâ el jawâb
of their   promised them   to give   answer

ʿala* mă, bihi ʿSâliḥ el memlece wa kair el̦ xaʿb el
according to the interest kingdom   good   plebs

ʿömoumiey.   * According to that wherein (is) the interest, etc.
common.

48. Yoqâl enna el ḥöcoumat el Fransêwieya qad uʿtemadat
    It is said that government   has resolved

en toxayyid mienâ ʿascerieya b'izê jezierat el Dirli,—aʿni,
to establish a harbour military opposite island   I mean

ma-bain Brest wa Xerbouj,—maʿ ʿamel maidân fesieḥ,
between   besides making area spacious

yomcinoh en yesêʿ arbaʿuin ʿelf jondiey.
which may possibly contain 40,000 soldier.

49. Yelouḥ   ennoh ʿSâr el uʿtumâd ʿala naʿsb Mousiou
    It is evident   the resolve to appoint Monsieur

Bandieni seficran fauq el ʿâda, wa moʿtemidan mofawwaẋan,
     ambassador beyond custom   trustee   entrusted

li daulat Fransê b'izê memlecet ITáliâ el jadieda ; wa
to govern^t *coram* kingdom   new

Mousiou Bicêrâ sefieran li ITáliâ fie Fransê.

    50. Inna ṣuḥḥat janâb sefier daulat   Ingilterra b'izê
            health of the Sire Ambassador of   *coram*

el bâb il Táli qad ittejehet   liḷ teqaddom ; wa yoqâl,
Porte High   has faced round towards*   advancing

ennoh se-yeʌheb   li tafyier il hewâ li'ejl   nawâl
that he will depart to change the air for the sake of attaining

ṣuḥḥatoh eḷ têmma.
his health   complete.   * Has taken a turn for the better.

    51. E'ḥad vâpourât el Messêjerie el Fransêwieya, el
            One of steamboats   Messagerie

mosemma' Prouisien [bi Rawiesien?] cên montazaran min Souria
named   Perousine ?   was expected from Syria

monʌ nehêr il iθnain el mâẕu. Wa mieTâdoh,   en
ever since Monday last.   its promise (of time) (was)

yeʌheb   θêni yeum ila Marsieliâ ; wa lil'ên lem yaṣul.
that it *go* 2nd day to   hitherto it has not arrived.

Wa ʌélic,   li ḥâdiθa   jarat   fie 'êletoh, fa
that (was), for an accident (which) happened in its engine

'ekkaratoh fie Rôdos. Wa'emma xalinoh, fa qad jâ' bihi
retarded it at Rhodes.   But its cargo,   came with it

el vâpour el Rousi, el mosemma' Xersonés.
the Russian steamer, named Chersonese.

52. Nawâḥu   Tesêlia   motemettiʿa bil hedou
    Borders (Tracts) of Thessaly (are) enjoying   repose
wa el râḥat el têmma, bi himme wa ʿunâyat Ḥaḏrat Ṣâḥub
    rest   complete,   care   providence   owner of
el daula wa el behê Ṭâyib Bâxa.
  lordship   brilliancy

53. Jelêlet melic el Swied, baʿd ziyâretoh Pâries, qad zêr
    Majesty   Sweden, after his visiting Paris had visited
mediena Londrâ, wa doʿa' lil ʿaxâ ʿand Ṣâḥub el semou, el
                was asked to supper   highness
Lôrd Palmerston.

54. Xâʿat   el akbâr ʿan moqâbala(tin)   se-taḥṣal
    Is diffused the news of a confronting,* *which* shall happen
fie mabain jelêlet Imperâʿöur Napôliôn, wa jelêlet melicet
    between his Majesty the Emperor   queen
Ispâniâ.   * A personal meeting.

55. Gazettet Bombây fie 27 Temouz aʿlanat, biʿenna el
hewa el aṣfar   qad fetec bi maqâʿaʿât moktelife fil Hind.
air yellow (*cholera*) had attacked districts divers   in India.

56. Yoqâl enna leis ittifâq bain Ḏabâʿ ul ʿumârat il
    It is said, that is no concord   officers   fleet
Fransêwieya wa Ḏabâʿ ul ʿumârat il Inglieziya ; liʿenna el
Fransêwieyien yoriedoun en yecounou wâḥdihom el Moḥamien
the French   wish   to be   alone they   Protectors
ʿan jeziera Madaqasqâr b'isrihê.
of island   collectively.

57. Qad ḥadaθat zelzele ʿaӡuima fie Antiegou fie Ameriecê:
fa hodimat hèᴀih el mediena: fa mât bihi min ᴀêlic ʿelfân
was demolished this city: died   from that 2000
nefsen.

58. El xiqâq lem yezel fie Ameriecê; wa lem tezel el
schism ceased not in
istiʿdâdât el ḥarbieya.
preparations warlike.

59. Inna ḥaӡrat ṣâḥub el ʿaӡama wa el iqtidâr,   maulâna
                        grandeur   authority,   our master
el solʿân el aʿӡam qad arsel ila el Ӡarb-a-kâna miqdâran
sultan   mightiest had dispatched   Mint   a quantity
wâfiran min ʿewâni el ᴀeheb wa el fuʎʎa, maʿ el ʿemr el
copious   vessels gold   silver   order
ʿâli bi Ӡarbihê ʿömlaten.
high to stamp them for coin.

60. Ceteb jornâl Ezmier fie 9 Ab:—Qad oʿlin   bi aʃwât
    Wrote journal   August: was notified by cries
el silâḥ,   nehêr el θelâθa, fie 6 Ab, ʿand el sêʿat el
"all'arme" (alarm) full day Tuesday   at   hour
ʿâxira mesê, ixtifâl el nâr fie ṣâyili el Islâm. Fa terâceʎ el
10ᵗʰ morning, activity of fire quarter   ran together
nês; lécin bil bâʿul cén ijtihêd li uʿfâihê: liʿenna
men: but in vain was the effort to extinguish it because
hoboub   riyâḥ el   ximâl ezêd   el lehieb, wa
blowing of the winds of the North increased the flame

esraṯ bi imtitêdoh: wa lâ sieyima li'enna el ʃâyiḥ, elleᴀi
hastened to extend it   especially   quarter wherein

naxabat bihi el nâr, cên jamieṯoh min el akʃâb, wa qarieba
shot (up)   the fire   all of it   planks (wood)   near

boyoutoh li baṯẊuhe [baṯẊ], naẓaran li Ẋaiqat
its houses to one another   in respect of the narrowness

eswâqoh wa xawâriṯhe. Fa cênet el moʃuiba ʿaẓuima, wa
of its streets and its roads.   was   calamity vast

el kisêra ṯömoumieya. Wa isteqâmat ehwâl el nâr tisṯa
loss   general   continued the terrors of the fire 9

sêṯât, doun en testaṯuiṯ ṯala teuquifihê qouwa baxarieya,
hours without that shall avail to stop it   force   human

naẓaran li sorṯat mesierihe ṯala janâḥ ul hewâ. Wa lemma jât
       speed of its march   wing   air.   when

el sêṯat el sêbiṯa min el ʃabâḥ, tewaqqafat el nâr, baṯdama cênet

daraset sebaṯataṯxar Ẋâḥuya(ten) wa ḥayan, taḥtewi ṯala
levelled   17   township   parish, (which) contain

sebaṯ mi'eya wa sebaṯuin beiten, wa θelêθa jawâmiṯ, wa
700   70   house   3   chief mosques

arbaṯa mesêjid, wa θelêθa medâris. Wa lau cênet laḥaqat
4   mosques   3   colleges   if it had reached

bi ʃâyiḥ el Yehoud, le mâ cên ʿair Allâh yaṯlem, ila 'ein
quarter   Jews,   none   save God   knows, whither

montchêhê. Wa qad auqaṯat hêᴀih el moʃuibat el morieṯa
its end.   has thrown down this calamity   awful

ecθar foqarâ ʿehl el Islâm bi Ḧâle moḦzine ; liʿenna ʿolouf
  poor people   state mournful   thousands

minhom, aʿsbaḦou bilâ meljaʿ, yesteʒulloun bil kiyâm, au
(who) passed morning refuge, shade themselves in tents

yaṭroẋoun wojouhehom li Ḧarr il xams.
expose   faces   heat   sun.

Rijâl el Ḧöcouma qad ṭamalou ma yajib ṭalaihom. Fa
Men of the Gov.t had done what was a duty

ṭasêcir el moḦâfaʒa wa el Ṭaupajieya wa baḦḦârât el sefâyin,
soldiers of garrison   artillery   crews   of ships

homma ixtafalou   bi himma,   yaqʿsar ṭanhe coll"
these   worked (were busy) earnestness falls short of it

medicḦ. Wa lâsieyima el wâli, Ṭoθmân Bâxâ, fa ittejeh bi
eulogy (nom.) especially Governor   set out by

nefsoh li maḦall il moʿsuiba, wa meceθ Ḧatte' el ʿSabâḦ.
himself place of calamity   tarried until   morning

    Waʿemma baḦḦârât el qabaq el Fransêwi Fôntounoui wa
    But the crews of ship of the line   Fontenoy ?

el vâpour Hêroun fa qad heraṭou ṭand ʒohour el Ḧarieqa maṭ
steamer   hurried at appearance of conflagration

ceθier min ẋabâyuṬhom, wa qaddamou kadâmât collieya ila
many of   officers   offered (gave) services entire to

el mediena, Ḧaseb xaṬârathom. Wa ce ᴧêlic ceθicroun min
the city,   cleverness.   so too   many   of

aͭyân el̦ tebaͭat el ajnabieya qad aʒherou jesêrathom bi
gentry   subjects   foreign   displayed bravery
teuqicf el̦ nâr, Ḧâl mesierhê.
stopping   during its progress.

61. Qad fotiḧ fie 6 Xobâͭ [1862] majlis el Parlemân fie
      was opened   February   assembly   in
Londrâ; wa telat jelêlet melicet Ingilterra fiehi koͭbathe el̦
London; read majesty queen   her address
senâwieya, toͭlin   bihe   sorourhe   wa irtiɮâhe min
annual   in which she declares her joy   satisfaction
ͭulâqâtihe maͭ qouwât Europpa el ajnabieyat, el leti lem
connections   powers of   foreign   which not
tezel moxaddada bi ribâͭ ul Ḧöbb. Wa θiqathe, bi ͭödm
ceased strung tight bond amity.   her trust (is) in non-
wojoud   sebab,   yestaͭuiͭ en yaɮörr bi ʒölḧ Europpa.
existence of cause (which) may be able to hurt peace of
Θomma tecellemat ͭan el̦ teswieyat il morɮuya el leti
Next   she spoke concerning settlement satisfactory which
jarat   maͭ Americce, bi köʒouʒ   Ḧâdiθat il̦ sefienat
took place with   in respect to the occurrence of the ship
il Inglieziеya; wa ͭan ittiḧâd il qouwât il̦ θclâθ fie mesielet
[the Trent]   agreement Powers Three   question
il Mecsiec; wa ͭan tejriedat il̦ ʒuin, wa axɾâl Marâcix.
  Mexico   expedition of China affairs of Morocco.

62. Ila' Ḧaɮrat* el moxtericien.   Bi coll^i sorour^{in}
     To Messieurs contributors (subscribers). With all joy

noqaddim el tehêni ila 'l jemieT bi dokoul hêʌe
we present congratulations to all on the entrance of this

el Tâm el jadied, sêʾilien el Maula', en yajTaloh
year new asking the Lord (Master) that he make it

Tâman mobâraeen, maqrounan bil teufieq wa 'l nejâh.
a year blessed coupled with prosperity and success.

NoTlin ila' ḤaẔrat el moxtericien fil Iscendaricya, enna
We notify to (our subscribers) in Alexandria that

hêʌe el Tadad faqaT, elleʌi hou auwal Tadad hêʌe el Tâm,
this numero only, which is first numero of this year

yaʒulhom min yed weeielina el kawâja Escender
will reach them from the hand of our agent Mr. Alexander

Toubeni: wa min baTdoh narjouhom, en yestelimou
henceforward we entreat them that they receive

jornâlêthom min wecêlêt el PosTa; liʾennena
their journals from the agencies of the Post because we

norsiloht† li coll¹ minhom râsen marraten maT el
dispatch *it* to all of them by the head, sometimes with the

Mescouvi, wa marraten maT el Fransêwi, ʾem el Nimsêwi.
Muscovite, sometimes with the French or Austrian.

63. Inna el moséhimien fil Tarieq bain Beirout wa
As regards the shareholders in (rail)way between

Damaxq, elleʌien el¹ên lem yadfaTou el qisT el θéliθ el
Damascus, who now have not paid instalment third

---

* ḤaẔrat, *presence*, used like Majesty, Excellency, as a title; but alike for the sovereign or for any respectable person.

† Jornâl, *masc.* though as a foreign word, it has *pl.* in -êt.

maTloub monᴀ xchr XobâT,   norsil   eshêmhom ila
demanded since month February we shall dispatch shares to

Baries,   lecei   tobâʔ   honêc bi moujib el mâdda 11,
Paris, in order that may be sold there by virtue of article

el moteʔalliqa bi ᴀêlic, min qawânien   el Xarâce;—iᴀe
relating to that (topic) of the canons (rules) Association if

lem   yadfaʔou hêᴀe el qisT min elˢên li Ḣadd 15
they (shall) not have paid this instalment   limit

Temouz el qâdim.
July   approaching.

Inna el mosêhimien, elleᴀien defaʔou el qosouT   li
As for the shareholders who have paid instalments up to

Ḣadd elˢân, yejib   Ḣoλourhom   min ibtidâ xehr
the present time, is right their personal presence   beginning

Temouz el qâdim ila maḢall   el Xarâce yeumieyan, min
July approaching,   place (office) the Company daily   from

el sêʔa 9 ila 11, li qabλ el fâyidat   el mosteḢaqqa lihom.
   hour   to get-in-hand interest (profit) due   to them.

CORRIGENDA.

Page 26, line 7, *for* xâmiqa *read* xâhiqa *or* xâmika.
,, 28, ,, 3, *for* Ṭâfi *read* Ṭafi.
,, 34, ,, 13, *for* Dar *read* Dâr.
,, 48, ,, 3, *for* Màu *read* Mán.
,, 111, ,, 7, *for* an adverb, *read* a preposition.
,, 115, ,, 15, *for* اخرام *read* اجرام.
,, 119, ,, 4, *for* Dimaxq, *read* Damaxq.
,, 136, ,, 4 from bottom, *for* Ircebt *read* Racebt.
,, 137, ,, 3, *for* Ṭileic *read* Ṭaleic.
,, 140, ,, 2, *for* sit, *read* set. (N.B.)
,, 147, ,, 5, *for* shall, *read* shalt.
,, 148, ,, 10, *for* does, *read* dost.
,, 155, ,, 3, *for* keif, *read* ceif. (N.B.)
,, 156, ,, 7, *omit* than.
,, 158, ,, 10, *for* qabla, *read* qablan.
,, 159, ,, 13, *for* ⁵emarac *read* ⁵emrec.
,, 159, ,, 3 from bottom, *for* weqt *read* waqt.

In many places I have failed of rightly placing the dot under *l* (of El), which a diligent student must correct. A zero would certainly catch the eye better. I may add that the typefounder has mounted ṭ on a taller stalk than I intended; and I now wish I had taken away the stalk entirely, and make the letter like a crescent-moon shield. Moreover, I wish ʃ to be only of the same height as *s*, and the small ∆ to be narrower than it is here.

Lightning Source UK Ltd.
Milton Keynes UK
UKHW040935201020
371904UK00001B/232